WORKS OF BERTOLT BRECHT

The Grove Press Edition

General Editor: Eric Bentley

Translators

Lee Baxandall

Eric Bentley

Martin Esslin

N. Goold-Verschoyle

H. R. Hays

Anselm Hollo

Christopher Isherwood

Frank Jones

Charles Laughton

Carl R. Mueller

Desmond I. Vesey

Richard Winston

Published Books

BERTOLT BRECHT

EDWARD II
A Chronicle Play

English Version and Introduction
by
ERIC BENTLEY

GROVE PRESS   NEW YORK

Originally published as *Leben Eduards des Zweiten von England* by Gustav Kiepenheuer Verlag A.G., Potsdam.

ISBN: 0-8021-5147-7

Library of Congress Catalog Card Number: 66-27698

Manufactured in the United States of America

Distributed by Random House, Inc., New York

GROVE PRESS, 841 Broadway, New York, NY 10003

10 9 8 7 6 5

CONTENTS

INTRODUCTION

BERTOLT BRECHT'S ONE TRAGEDY?

If Brecht's early works have been neglected and under-rated, *Edward II* must surely be the most neglected and underrated of them all. I was told by several persons that they assumed the play would not turn up at all in an English-language edition of Brecht's works "since it is a translation from the English, and who wants to have Marlowe translated back from the German?" My reply is that the same point was made, earlier, about *The Three-penny Opera,* with as little justification. Brecht was un-interested in translation and probably incapable of it. Anything he touched became inalienably his own. It is true that he was prepared to lift many lines from other authors, not to mention incidents, but even lines and incidents reproduced by Brecht without change are always utterly changed by their new context. The work of other authors was infinitely suggestive for Brecht, but *what* it suggested was entirely his own affair, and would have surprised those other authors very much indeed.

Even when people are told that Brecht's treatment of Marlowe's *Edward II* is "free," what they expect is Mar-lowe cut and edited, as by an expert stage director or schol-arly popularizer who aims at providing the "essence of Mar-lowe." Possibly Brecht uses almost as much of Marlowe's plot as that kind of adaptor, and quotes almost as many of the lines, yet his aim, to realize which he has to write in many lines of his own, and invent new incidents, is diametrically opposed. Telling a tale that is only outwardly —and not at all points even outwardly—the same, he tells it about quite different people to the end of embodying quite a different theme and communicating quite a different vision of life. The remarkable thing is how much of the original can be absorbed in what is essentially a brand-new play. An aspect of Brecht's genius for which he has not yet been given full credit is his gift of assimilation. How many fruits he sucked dry! This is not to say it was a matter of indifference what fruit came his way. To speak less metaphorically, the material must be transformable, but must also, in its as yet untransformed state, have something substantial to offer. And Brecht had an uncanny way of finding what offered him most, whether it was a particular Japanese Nō or a play by Marlowe that few Germans had even heard of. Which, no doubt, is yet another aspect of his genius.

What was it that Marlowe's play did offer him? Many things, a number of which will emerge as we proceed. What first comes to mind is the subject—a Brechtian one—of a homosexual relationship seen as a fatal infatuation, seen, moreover, as masochistic in relation to the male principal and as sadistic in relation to women. Secondly, the form. Speaking on general lines, one would have to say, first, that the form of an Elizabethan chronicle play offered Brecht that distance from immediate experience which later he would bring under the heading of *Verfremdung,* or alienation. England in the Middle Ages is, in other words, another of his exotic-grotesque pseudo-milieus. Thinking specifically of Marlowe's *Edward II* one would want to add that it has a remarkably expressive pattern of action which can be taken over and perhaps in some respects improved upon. According to this pattern, the hero becomes a more sympathetic person as his fortunes grow worse, while his chief antagonist becomes more and more repellent as he has more and more success.

If that—plus, shall we put it? a lot of usable incidents and lines—is what Marlowe had to offer Brecht, of what did the Brechtian transformation consist? Anyone interested in the technique of playmaking—the carpentry of it, as it were—might learn much from watching the young Brecht reduce the number of characters from about forty to about twenty and simplifying the incidents to match this reduction. In one who was only just starting out as a playwright, the technical achievement alone was enough to mark him as a dramatic genius. But probably little of this simplifying was done for its own sake: Brecht had no objection to a bewildering complexity, as his other plays of this period show. The point—as with his more famous transformations of later years—was to turn things completely around, to write a counter-play, to *re*-write Marlowe, to correct him, to stand him (if one may adapt what Marx said of his own relation to Hegel) on his feet.

A reader of Marlowe who starts to read the Brecht is surprised and perhaps disappointed very early on by Brecht's omission of the most famous purple patch in the play, Gaveston's speech about the fun which he and Edward will have together:

> I must have wanton poets, pleasant wits,
> Musicians, that with touching of a string
> May draw the pliant king which way I please:
> Music and poetry is his delight,
> Therefore I'll have Italian masks by night,
> Sweet speeches, comedies, and pleasing shows,
> And in the day, when he shall walk abroad,
> Like sylvan nymphs my pages shall be clad;
> My men, like satyrs grazing on the lawns,
> Shall with their goat-feet dance an antic hay;
> Sometime a lovely boy, in Dian's shape,
> With hair that gilds the water as it glides,
> Crownets of pearl about his naked arms,
> And in his sportful hands an olive tree,
> To hide those parts which men delight to see,
> Shall bathe him in a spring . . .

If the topic is homosexuality, would not such a passage seem highly relevant? Reading on, one finds that it is not relevant—is not *possible*—to the experience Brecht depicts, the world he creates. A whole dimension of the poet Marlowe is not usable, and it may well be the dimension which most of his English-language readers find the most attractive: Renaissance sensuousness finding expression in luxurious words and sinuous rhythms.

Brecht's refusal of the Marlovian line is not motivated by modesty. The Brechtian counter-play is always a sort of serious parody, converting the sublime to the grotesque. In Marlowe, the steady roll of the blank verse has an effect comparable in solemnity to the rhymed Alexandrines of French classical tragedy. The Brecht version intersperses iambic pentameter with shorter lines—and sometimes with longer ones—that break the pattern and shatter, as it were, the icon. As with the form, so with the content. The homosexuality in Marlowe is at once esthetic and ambiguous. Sometimes seeming conscious, physical, and even animal, it seems at other times but the Elizabethan cult of poeticized friendship. When the elder Mortimer says Edward will get over it soon, we aren't compelled to disbelieve him. As for Brecht, some readers have had the impression that he wanted to "juice up" the material, providing, as it were, a bridge between Christopher Marlowe and American "homosexual literature" of the 1960's. That is not the point. It is not even true. Whereas Marlowe's Gaveston is seen not just as bedfellow but even more as royal "favorite," and a marriage we need not regard as phony is being arranged for him with a princess, Brecht's Gaveston is a sexual partner first and last. The word "whore" is bound to recur, as it does, if, as we do, we keep hearing what his enemies think of him.

Actually, a reader who looked at the end of the play first, even though there is no sex in it, would receive the same jolt from Brecht's changes as the reader who looks at the opening scenes. When Marlowe's Edward has to give up not only Gaveston but this world, what he is

left with is the Christian religion, i.e., the hope of a *next*
world. His friend Baldock provides the cue:

> Make for a new life, man; throw up thy eyes
> And heart and hand to heaven's immortal throne . . .

And so the lyric afflatus prompted in the beginning by
sex is sustained in the end by religious sentiment:

> Yet stay a while, forbear thy bloody hand,
> And let me see the stroke before it comes
> That even then when I shall lose my life
> My mind may be more steadfast on my God . . .

And:

> I am too weak and feeble to resist.
> Assist me, sweet God, and receive my soul.

Now, though Brecht's Edward also ends up as a meta-
physician, the metaphysics are the opposite of Christian
—precisely the opposite, indeed, a very travesty of Chris-
tianity (close in its wording to an acknowledged parody
Brecht wrote on the subject, the "Grand Hymn of Thanks-
giving"):

> Therefore
> Who is dark, let him stay dark,
> Who is unclean, let him stay unclean.
> Praise deficiency, praise cruelty, praise
> The darkness.   (p. 88)

And we find, in this ending, an instance of the same
words coming to mean the opposite when used by Brecht.
I refer to Mortimer's summing up, his speech about the
wheel of fortune. In Marlowe's play this Elizabethan
commonplace concerning the fate of "magistrates" is not
felt to be contradicted by an affirmative treatment of young
Edward's accession to the throne: by a turn of fortune's
wheel Mortimer gets his deserts, but the accession of

Edward III is an improvement and a purification. Brecht
on the other hand, through Mortimer, directs the argument
against the new king, as much as to say: Your turn will
come. Here, the wheel of fortune is an image of a phi-
osophy that hovers over the whole play: history goes
meaninglessly round and round.

Luckily, it is not the only philosophy in the play, or it
would reduce all the characters to mere pawns on a
historical chess board. No one could see or read Brecht's
Edward II and feel that this is what they are. Brecht's
Edward is far less passive than Marlowe's. This is indeed
Brecht's most decisive divergence from his source, and
it is in looking further into it that we begin to discover
what Brecht put into the play to make up for the Marlovian
elements which he so drastically cut. Whether he came
out with a play which is better than Marlowe's or worse
is, I think, a question not to be asked: their plays are,
finally, so different as to be incommensurable. But I do
think that, like many another great play, Marlowe's has
shortcomings and that Brecht sometimes found solutions
where his predecessor had found none. This much by way
of explanation, if what follows gives the impression that
I do consider Brecht's a better play.

Marlowe's eloquence has rightly been praised, yet there
is something about his eloquent *Edward II* that is dra-
matically unsatisfying. "Edward sings too many arias,"
one tends to say. Yet the fact that he does serves to con-
ceal a dramatic weakness, which derives from Edward's
passivity. Thinking about the shortcomings of Marlowe's
play, one recalls W. B. Yeats' rejection of passive suffer-
ing as a dramatic subject. And whether or not it should
be rejected out of hand, it certainly presents problems
which are seldom solved. Looking at this particular nar-
rative, one finds two nodal points in it: the point where
Edward gives Gaveston up, and the point where he gives
the crown up. Both are actions which are not actions.
That's Edward, Marlowe might have said. It is a proposi-

tion which is reversed by Brecht, whose Edward refuses
to give up either Gaveston or the crown. He loses them
anyway, of course; so, from a cynical point of view,
there's no difference between the two Edwards. There
is all the difference in the world from a tragic point of
view—and is not *Edward II* the one play of Brecht's which
can be called a tragedy in any accepted sense?

However this may be, we are confronted here with
opposite characters in opposite stories. One play is about
a weak man who, under pressure, gives up his friend
first and his crown later, and interests us only in his
very human weakness and by virtue of the faint halo that
is cast around it by all the grace and poeticizing. The other
is a play about an infatuated man, made palatable to us in
the beginning by no poetry or charm, but earning our
admiration, gradually and with difficulty, by a surprising
loyalty both to his friend and to his idea of himself as
king. Marlowe's play, for all its magnificent rhetoric, is a
little monotonous because Edward for so long stays the
same, repeating himself not only in words but in action (or
rather in inaction). Though the young Brecht is often
spoken of as mainly a lyric poet, nothing marks him more
unmistakably as a dramatic genius than the way in which
he was able to make Edward change not just at the end
but throughout the play. We already see a different Edward
in the middle of the play when we find him toughened
by a soldier's life in the open. That is of course only the
outward form and result of a toughness which, Brecht
makes us realize, must have been always there. It is not
out of a clear sky, then, that Edward, facing his worst and
final sufferings, proves strong and serene:

> ... such water hardens my limbs: which are now
> Like cedar wood.
> The stench of excrement gives me boundless greatness!
> And the good sound of the drum keeps me awake,
> Though weak, so death won't find me fainting but
> Waking.   (p. 87)

Now, if one had to illustrate Marlowe's gift of character creation from *Edward II,* one could not say very much about any character save Edward himself. If Brecht eliminated about twenty of Marlowe's figures, he did so in order to develop more fully the four leading *personae,* who, after Edward, are Gaveston, the Queen, and Mortimer. I have already tried to suggest what he made of Gaveston. To that broad suggestion should be added that Gaveston is here given further touches of reality that belong to the situation of a young man who has not so much worked hard to get a great personage's attention as he has had this attention forced upon him:

> I . . . do not know
> What it was about me of too much or too little
> That made this Edward, now the king,
> Unable to leave me alone,
> For my own mother found nothing in me
> Any different from the extremely
> Usual, no goiter, no white skin . . .   (p. 16)

Because Edward is really infatuated, Gaveston does not have to be a seducer or even a schemer, and the pattern is more human, more typical and, finally, more dramatic this way. The downfall of Gaveston has the more poignancy because it is so much more than he "asked for."

If Gaveston, in the Brecht, is less the standard wastrel, the Queen is far less shadowy. It is remarkable how skillfully the young Brecht was able to mark the stages in this character's development. Whereas in Marlowe the Queen's liaison is suddenly there, and mentioned, in the Brecht we see it happen step by step, and feel the inexorable logic of it. The drama in the material is found by underlining her reluctance on the one hand and Edward's aggressive misogyny on the other. (The dynamics of homosexuality —hence its drama—are always better seen in the sadistic and masochistic components than in the actual attraction-by-the-same-sex.) Again, there is great technical accomplishment in the modern play, but, again, that is subordinate to a larger human matter: in this case, the Queen's gradual loss of all sense of herself and, therewith, of reality generally. Nowhere is Brecht's audacity more marked or, to my mind more triumphant, than in the scene entitled: "Queen Anne laughs at the world's emptiness." No topic, of course, has been more often dilated upon by modern writers than this "emptiness of the world." Credit is due to Brecht, not for taking up the subject, but for showing in a succession of dramatic encounters how the Queen *discovers* the void.

In Marlowe, Edward has but one partner and foil: Gaveston. In Brecht, he has three: Gaveston, the Queen, and Mortimer. The contrast is a strong one between the infatuated, stubborn king and the lost, embarrassed, not stupid, but fundamentally rather innocent boy friend. The contrast is strong, too, between Edward and his queen. Though this Edward has been able to become a father, everything else we know of him seems homoerotic. Gaveston is not the whole story. Even in his isolation, later, Edward is the man's man, finding strength on horseback and in the tent, an aging Hippolytus. And even the asexuality of his final phase is part of the complex. The Queen, on the other hand, is "all woman." She will be loyal to her man as long as she is allowed to be, but when this loyalty is mocked and, as it were, forbidden, she will drift to another man. There is a convincing morbidity in this drift as Brecht shows it, since it is a drift to her former man's principal enemy and opposite.

Principal enemy and opposite: that is why Mortimer is the principal partner among Edward's three. And therein lies another achievement of Brecht's. Marlowe's play suffers because his Edward has no adequate partner once Gaveston drops out in the middle. In Brecht's play Gaveston is less important from the start than Mortimer, and so is the more expendable. If all four characters are mostly Brecht's own inventions, Mortimer is ninety-nine percent

so. Marlowe's Young Mortimer is in the beginning just a
barbaric young man who is capable of having at Gaveston
with his sword to cap an argument. We feel he takes over
the Queen only because that's what barbarians do. It is
Brecht's idea that Mortimer was a scholar, and has to be
won from his books before he enters the political arena
at all. More original still, his meditations have already led
him to Solomon's conclusion: all is vanity. What for the
Queen is a destination was for him a point of departure.
The absolute "nullity of human things and deeds"—what
a premise for political action! The conception permits
Brecht to create, in the first instance, an effectively tragi-
comic scoundrel and, in the second, to define the perfect
antithesis to Edward: Edward is the man of feeling,
Mortimer of reason. But so long as the contrast remains
so general it has little human interest or dramatic force.
These it derives from an "action" that gives it concrete
expression and by further "interpretation" of what reason
and feeling, in this context, signify. Mortimer remarks
that Edward "Antaeus-like . . . draws strength from the
soil." Antaeus was the son of the Earth Mother, and
Edward himself says:

> Dull-eyed, you Mortimers do arithmetic, and
> Burrow in books like worms.
> But in books there is nothing about Edward who
> Reads nothing, does not do arithmetic,
> Knows nothing, and has intimate ties with Nature.
> He's nourished by quite different food.   (p. 43)

One thinks of poems, novels, or plays in which Nature and
Reason confront each other and are both benign. Nature
can for example, imply a utopia of noble savages; Reason
can be the law of a God who is all-wise and all-good. In
the world of the young Brecht, such benignities have all
been replaced by horrors of disenchantment. Some bizarre
but solid paradoxes result. For example, the "Nature" of

Edward is precisely what for the world at large passes for
*un*natural:

> Oh, Spencer, since words are rough,
> And only part us heart from heart
> And understanding is not granted to us,
> Amid the deafness nothing remains except
> Bodily contact between men . . .   (p. 55)

Conversely, the "Reason" of Mortimer is hardly that of the
optimistic rationalist. At best it is that of some of the
French existentialists who see the whole universe as hostile
and Reason as the element that, if you're lucky, reduces
the hostility to temporarily manageable proportions. The
final paradox is a certain fundamental agreement between
Edward and Mortimer. Both see the world as impossible
but suggest the hope that it may at times become "possible" if we appeal to what is most human in us. What
they disagree about is the character of our humanity,
Mortimer finding it in reason, Edward in feeling, which—
in Brecht's context—makes of the former a Machiavellian
or even fascistic politician, and of the latter . . . a homosexual. Obviously, from the point of view of almost any
conceivable modern theatre public, this whole story is
"beyond good and evil."

A minor character in Marlowe's play compares Gaveston to Helen of Troy:

> Monster of men,
> That, like the Greekish strumpet, train'd to arms
> And bloody wars so many valiant knights . . .

Brecht, who at any point can take what one Marlowe
character says and give it to some other character, not
only gives this comparison to Mortimer, but makes of
it the longest and perhaps most important speech of the
play, a sort of centerpiece for the whole drama. From it
we learn that such a relationship as that of Helen and

Paris or Gaveston and Edward is the source of human trouble, but not because society considers it immoral. It makes no difference to Mortimer "whether Helen was a whore/Or had a score of healthy grandchildren." It is simply that "the ear of reason had . . . been stopped up" (p. 19). In other words Mortimer offers himself and his own philosophy as the nearest the world can come to any solution. His opposite, Edward, represents the worst that the world can know: infatuation, i.e., surrender to pure feeling.

At bottom, Mortimer's philosophy is less paradoxical than contradictory, for if we believe him when he tells us the world is nothing, we are hardly disposed to take him up on it when he offers to save that world from passion. The poet is able to indicate by the tone of Mortimer's speeches that they can scarcely be accepted at face value:

> Because a few hats are off and on the ground
> Before a son of a bitch, the English people
> Push their island over the precipice.   (p. 12)

Well, any tears Mortimer sheds over this prospect are crocodile tears, since disaster is for him normal and natural and inevitable, and, in the play, we know this without even going through the logical reasoning, since Mortimer, though not the usual villain, is still the villain.

And Edward, though not the usual hero, is still a hero. This story is, if you like, yet another of those modern defenses of the sensitive homosexual destroyed by a cruelly hostile world, and can be confidently recommended to the broad public such stories apparently command. If at bottom Mortimer's philosophy is contradictory, if his rationalism is finally irrational and his reason unreasonable, Edward's antirational view, the world being what it is, is rational.

> Amid the deafness nothing remains except
> Bodily contact between men.

If the Trojan War was as mad and meaningless as, say, World War I, then isn't it possible that what Paris and Helen did in bed was the only part of the whole transaction that had any human value or even much human substance? Whatever you and I, in the context of our own lives, make of this question, isn't it cogent for Edward, in the context of Brecht's play, to answer the comparable question in the positive: the relationship between Edward and Gaveston—not seen "poetically" as by Marlowe but in all its physicality—provided something to hold on to, which is more than could be said for anything else that transpires in the play, with a single exception I shall revert to in a moment.

Brecht's brilliant, complicated dialectic is seen in the endings to which Mortimer and Edward come, which are "the same" but also "the opposite." Both men end quietly, accept their end philosophically. There is something stoical, and hence traditionally tragic, about both endings. Mortimer's is the more ostentatiously so (he has two big speeches, the bull speech, and the wheel of fortune speech), and the ostentation "gives the show away," that is, gives away that he *is* putting on a show. He enacts the very parody of a hero's death. That he is really *un*heroic is clear in that he closes with a taunt toward the young king. Edward's heroism is genuine, and his power to endure is that other "something to hold on to" which I just mentioned.

Heroic courage is the tragic virtue, and Edward has it. Mortimer's courage, if we take it to exist at all, is unheroic because it needs to be propped by hatred and cynicism: it is easier to die if you are spitting hatred against others all the while and if you truly find all living worthless anyway. (Hence the abundant unheroic courage of modern

militarists.) Not the least interesting feature of Brecht's
Mortimer is that he has known this all along:

> . . . frightened like one burned to death,
> I wrap myself in the skin of another man:
> This butcher's son.   (p. 29)

Here, quite early in the action, Mortimer thinks of the
skin of Gaveston as a cloak in which he can hide. Our
strong man is weak. Our courageous man is unheroic.

I have indicated that what makes a hero out of Edward
in Brecht's play is, in the first instance, that, unlike
Marlowe's protagonist, he *can* say No. His two refusals,
spaced out in the way they are, do much to give the play
its grand and cogent structure. Edward can say No because
he possesses the primordial, Promethean tragic virtue of
sheer endurance. The effect and meaning of this is much
heightened by Brecht, because he gives Edward much
more to endure. Less etherially poetic, the Brecht play is
far more brutal than the Marlowe. If some of the more
external barbarities (like bringing on Mortimer's head)
are discarded, far more real torture is inflicted. At times
the story itself is changed to this end. For example, it is
Brecht's doing that Edward had the chance to save
Gaveston and missed it, giving Mortimer his chance to
turn his knife in the psychological wound:

>   had you
> Not drowned their words out with your drums
> Had not, that is, too little confidence
> And too much passion, too swift anger
> Troubled your eye, your favorite Gaveston
> Would be still alive.   (p. 43)

As for the sequence where Edward is asked to abdicate,
Brecht not only changes the action to a refusal to abdicate,
but also makes it essentially a contest between Edward
and Mortimer. (In Marlowe's abdication scene, Mortimer
is not even present.) This contest has the character of a

cat-and-mouse game. While the cruder tortures of the Gurneys are mostly kept off-stage, the pressure inflicted by Mortimer upon Edward's spirit—Mortimer's attempt to brainwash him, if you will—is all presented and is of the very essence of this play.

If the tale of Edward's imprisonment and death is mostly taken from Marlowe, who had mostly taken it from Holinshed, Brecht's changes are still considerable, and underline both Edward's final victory and the horror of the conditions which failed to defeat him.

> The dungeon where they keep me is the sink
> Wherein the filth of all the castle falls . . .
> And there in mire and puddle have I stood . . .

That is Marlowe. Holinshed had spoken of "a chamber over a foul filthy dungeon full of dead carrion" but Brecht paints a picture which is not only more revolting than Marlowe and Holinshed but belongs to a different pattern and intention. Where his Edward stands is nothing more nor less than the cloaca, and we see him there actually steeped in excrement and presumably continuing to be shat and pissed on before our eyes. So ends Edward the playboy. The Baalian quester for pleasures, for anal pleasures, ends in the sewer. It would be a mistake to consider the young Brecht merely fascinated by filth, though he may *also* have been fascinated by it. There is dramatic appropriateness, and irony, in Edward's final condition. For one thing it is very close to the primal condition, the situation of the human being born *inter urinas et faeces*. And it is not just that Edward finds himself there, but that there he achieves strength and even serenity.

Edward II is, then, in its own Schopenhauerian way, a heroic tragedy, and as such is unique in the lifework of Brecht. For while he would often portray courageous action and the self-sacrifice it entails—as with his Kattrin, the son in *The Mother,* the revolutionaries of *Days of the Commune,* etc., etc.—the context of the later heroism is imposed by the author's optimistic progressivism, which negates tragedy as traditionally accepted. Edward's heroism belongs to the category of the traditionally tragic in that it is not utilitarian but serves only (only!) to demonstrate that man is not a worm.

Of course, for Brecht personally, there is a continuing thread from this early hero of his to the truly "positive heroes" found here and there in his later works. It is to be found in that ability to say No which for Brecht had such very urgent importance. For this there are clear historical reasons, notably the inability of his own people, the Germans, to say No to the Mortimers of the Nazi Party. "Will none of you say NO?" cries the chorus before the last scene of Brecht's chronicle of life under the Nazis, while the scene itself ends on the decision to issue an anti-Nazi pamphlet consisting of the one word No. Conversely (the word is needed often in expounding the works of the great dramatic dialectician) the person who cannot say No is a constantly recurring figure of the Brecht œuvre. He is depicted most flat-footedly in the poem "On Giving This World One's Endorsement" which depicts and denounces the average fellow-traveler of Nazism. He receives his classical definition in Galy Gay of A Man's A Man. And he gets subtle, two-sided, no doubt dialectical, and possibly ambiguous treatment in Herr Keuner, Mother Courage, Schweyk, Galileo, and Azdak.

Perhaps Edward II should make us rethink the whole topic of Brecht's development. Generally all the early plays are lumped together as negative in spirit, and in them the men who can't say No are spotted and reported on by the critics. Actually, for all the despair that floats free in these plays, they frequently bear witness to a kind of human strength. In his recent introduction to Drums in the Night, Frank Jones makes us aware that Kragler is one of Brecht's strong men. If we had not noticed it, it is because we take his abandonment of the revolution as irreclaimably "negative." No doubt the later Brecht wanted the Kraglers of this world to be disapproved of, but the Brecht who wrote *Drums in the Night* presented Kragler's achieving of independence as positive.

It is interesting that in Brecht's plays the men of sheer action are generally bad, whereas good actions tend to come, if at all, from people who have hitherto been markedly passive. Whereas the men of action in *Mother Courage* keep busy slaughtering people, good actions get performed after long preparation by persons who were so gentle they seemed till then quite inactive, such as Swiss Cheese and Kattrin. If the passive people of the early plays never become doers-of-good, the principal ones do shake themselves out of their passivity: Kragler, for example, at the end of *Drums,* and Garga at the end of *Jungle of Cities.* Baal is characterized, on the one hand, by an extreme passivity, yet on the other is a sort of non-spiritual Don Quixote in quest of happiness. Perhaps only *A Man's A Man* is a study of complete inability to say No, and even there the joke, in the original version, is that once Galy Gay is reconstructed he becomes a Leader: he has moved from the camp of the amiably passive to that of the brutally active. At any rate, when the young Bertolt Brecht chose Marlowe's *Edward II* as the basis for a play, one could only have supposed that he chose it as one of the classic studies of passivity and weakness, and one could only have expected he was himself interested in presenting to the world a man who couldn't say No. That he presented a man who *could* say No, and this long before he heard any talk about "positive heroes" or even studied Marxism, should give certain of his critics pause.

Close to all the other early plays, *Edward II* is especially close to *Jungle of Cities* and *A Man's A Man.* All three dramatize a contrast between two men, depict a struggle between two men, and in similar terms. It is a question of the actual or virtual rape of one by the other, and it is a question of the masochistic pleasure which the raped one takes in the rape. "It was the best time," as

Garga succinctly puts it, after being seduced and taken over by Shlink. In *A Man's A Man* Galy Gay is "raped" by the British army in the form of a machine-gun unit, but the character contrast is with Bloody Five upon whose quest to identify him *as* Galy Gay, not Jeraiah Jip, the story is built; and by a very suggestive quirk Bloody Five speaks at one point of the possibility of raping Galy Gay. However, the contrast is almost wholly in terms of the active-passive elements, rather than hetero-homo.

In Marlowe's *Edward II,* one could believe that the King was seduced by Gaveston. What we notice first about Brecht's rendering is that the responsibility rests more with the king, who is infatuated, while Gaveston preserves a degree of detachment. But the Brechtian "rape" is no more directly sexual in this play than in *A Man's A Man.* It is again a military rape. The rapist is neither the king nor Gaveston but Mortimer. And Brecht reworks the plot to give the king's part in this relationship a decisive and unmistakable masochism. Where in Marlowe, Mortimer simply escapes, in Brecht he is released by the king for no clear reason. The reason is *made* clear by the subsequent action and, more specifically, by the king when questioned about it later:

> . . . I spared Mortimer for the wicked pleasure
> It gave me to do just that.   (p. 59)

Sparing Mortimer gave pleasure, in the first instance, for its sheer arbitrariness: the king did it for "the hell of it," "for kicks." But what hell, and what was it that did the kicking? Surely the part of Edward which wanted his enemy to win—that is, the part of Edward which wanted to lose. To the sad logic of the old tragic tale from Holinshed and the old tragic drama of Marlowe, Brecht adds a further kind of doom: a psycho-logic. It entails, incidentally, transferring the homosexuality to Mortimer, for not only is Mortimer drawn very dynamically into a close relation with Edward, he desires Edward's wife, a fact which, in this context, must be taken as homosexual girl-sharing. Here *Edward II* is close to *Baal*.

Brecht's tragedy has a puritanic aspect. His hero has been a heterosexual before the play opens; becomes a homosexual later; and, later still, withdraws, through friendship, and, even more, through friendship betrayed, into heroic solitude. At the end he is almost a saint. The role of Mortimer has a precisely contrary movement. He begins in bookish isolation and then plunges headlong into Edward's world. When he takes over the Queen he is, as it were, having Edward's hetero- and homosexual phases at the same time, and this fact is presented in what may strike the reader as an Elizabethan rather than a Brechtian vein, namely, as morally heinous. Yet, if such puritanism seems a far cry from the pansexuality propagated by the character Baal, the play of *Baal* also bears witness to much sexual nausea, to much hatred of sex and therefore much fear of sex, and what is perhaps the finest lyric in the play proposes a romantic, asexual purity as an alternative:

> He dreams at times about a little meadow
> A patch of blue in the sky and nothing more.

While a first impression of Brecht's *Edward II* may make us say how much "more sex" there is in it than in Marlowe's play, the point of the sex is not sex itself. A vulgarized Freudianism, which finds sex hidden at the bottom of everything, would be the worst of all critical philosophies to bring to a play in which the surface itself is all sex and at the bottom is . . . what? My metaphor itself smacks too much of popular Freudianism. Literary subject matter cannot always be neatly split into manifest and latent. In *Edward II* it is less a question of sex concealing something else than of its being part of a larger whole, part of a human fate which is a sexual fate but not exclusively so. Hence, while Edward's relation with Gaveston is more blatantly sexual than it had been for

Marlowe, that does not prevent the poet Brecht from
finding in it an image of a fate that is not just sexual:

> Against the hour when the corpse is found
> Prepare a worthy grave. But do
> Not hunt for him.
> He's like the man who walks into the woods
> And the bushes grow up thick behind him and
> The plants shoot up again and
> The thicket's got him.
>   (p. 43)

One cannot ask that a theatre audience that sees *Edward II*
should have read Brecht's "Ballad of Friendship," his
"Ballad of Cortez' Men," and his "The Song of the Fort
Donald Railroad Gang" in order to feel more at home
with such a treatment of the theme. Perhaps indeed the
passage just quoted is more powerful if it comes as an
astonishment. Of a sudden we then see Gaveston as part
of that vast organism, Nature, to which Edward acknowl-
edges so close a relation. A self-devouring organism:
Gaveston was part of it and is swallowed up by it. Specifically by a *thicket*. The word is the same as in the title
of *Im Dickicht der Städte*. And for all the jungle beasts,
tigers, wolves, or wild bulls, that haunt *Edward II*, a
Dickicht is, incidentally, not a jungle: only density of
vegetation is implied, not the presence of wild animals.
Edward pictures a Gaveston, not torn to pieces by beasts,
but stifled by the under- and overgrowth. And it is soon
as if he had never been: what flourish are the grasses, the
plants, and the trees. The image is cosmic rather than
clinical.

Even Edward's final triumph over sex should not be
taken as the farthest reach of the poet's imagination in this
play. This heroism is more than a new-found chastity.
The chastity is itself but an aspect of something else:
independence. Edward had not been able to do without
Gaveston. He had not been able to do without the Queen
even when he insulted and rejected her: a contradiction

she spotted and taunted him with. He could not do without his last loyal retainers until the chief one proved *disloyal* and betrayed him. (The Baldock episode is another brilliant innovation of Brecht's.) It is only when he *is* without all these people he "could not do without" that Edward finds he not only can do without them, but that he is now a man, he is now himself, for the first time. He is like a hypochondriac cripple who does not discover he can stand upright and walk without assistance until his crutches have been brutally torn from him.

It has been remarked, it could hardly not be, that *Brecht's plays present victimization,* and many have got the impression that his early plays show and represent a mere wallowing in it. But this is to see what one might call the primary movement of the action and not the counter-movement that ensues and for the sake of which the play was written. *Each of these plays is actually a cry of: Don't fence me in!* Baal may be cruelly left to perish, but he has lived, and under the open sky: he didn't let them fence him in. Kragler wouldn't be fenced in even by an ideology which the author of *Drums in the Night* would—much later—accept. (That is, of course, not all he wouldn't be fenced in by.) *Jungle of Cities* ends as Garga breaks loose from Chicago itself, the cage in which the whole action had been enclosed. The paradox of Edward's final posture is that he is physically fenced in but spiritually liberated. There is nothing more they can do to him, and this in two senses: that he cannot suffer worse humiliations and, secondly, that his fearlessness is an iron barrier which they cannot cross: he has fenced *them* in. In each case Brecht shows a man giving way to pressure, and hence exhibiting human weakness, but in each case there comes the counter-movement: the worm turns, the weak man shows strength, and the ending is in some sense a victory. Even Galy Gay, in the original conception, not the Marxized version, is getting his own back at the end. "He'll have our heads yet," say those who once had called him "a man who can't say No." These endings are not pious, renewing our faith in human goodness, while the sun comes up at the back, and soft music plays. That kind of ending stands rebuked by the young Brecht. But so does a kind of ending he was more likely to have had in mind: the ending of the typical naturalistic play in which life is simply too much for pathetic little Homo sapiens and someone jumps in a lake at the bottom of the garden or shoots himself in the next room.

—Eric Bentley

EDWARD II

This play I wrote with Lion Feuchtwanger.
—Bertolt Brecht

CHARACTERS

KING EDWARD II
QUEEN ANNE, *his wife*
KENT, *his brother*
YOUNG EDWARD, *his son, later Edward III*
GAVESTON
ARCHBISHOP OF WINCHESTER
ABBOT OF COVENTRY, *later Archbishop of Winchester*
MORTIMER
LANCASTER
RICE AP HOWELL
BERKELEY
SPENCER
BALDOCK
THE ELDER GURNEY
THE YOUNGER GURNEY
LIGHTBORN
JAMES

PEERS, SOLDIERS, A BALLAD PEDDLER, A MONK

Here is publicly presented the history of the troublesome
      reign of Edward II, King of England, and his
      lamentable death
Also the fortune and end of his favorite, Gaveston
Further, the confused fate of Queen Anne
Likewise the rise and fall of the great earl, Roger Mortimer
All of which happened in England, chiefly in London,
      six hundred years ago.

*14 December 1307: Return of the favorite Danyell Gaves-
ton for the coronation of Edward II.*

London.

GAVESTON (*reading a letter from King Edward*):
    "My father, the elder Edward, is dead. Fly here,
        Gaveston, and share England with your bosom
        friend King Edward II."
    I've come. These lines of love from you
    Have whisked the brig across from Ireland.
    The city of London, for this banished man,
    Is Heaven to a soul that's just got there.
    My father used to say to me: at eighteen
    You're fat already from drinking too much ale.
    My mother used to say:
    Fewer people will follow your hearse
    Than hens have teeth. And now a king
    Grabs at a chance of friendship with her son!
    Hullo, there! Reptiles!
    Who is the first one, crawling in my path?

    TWO PERSONS *enter*.

FIRST:
    Men who would like to serve your lordship.

GAVESTON:
   What can you do?
FIRST:
   I can ride.
GAVESTON:
   But I don't have a horse. How about you?
SECOND:
   Soldier. Served in the war against Ireland.
GAVESTON:
   But I don't have a war. So God be with you, sirs.
SECOND:
   God?
FIRST (*to the* SECOND):
   England pays nothing for old soldiers, friend.
GAVESTON:
   England provides St. James's Hospital.
FIRST:
   Where a fellow can kick the bucket.
GAVESTON:
   To kick the bucket is the soldier's fate.
SECOND:
   It is, is it?
   Then may you croak, yourself, in this England!
   And may you fall by a soldier's hand!

   Both leave.

GAVESTON (*alone*):
   Sounds just like my father. Well!
   Should a goose pretend to be a porcupine
   And stick its feathers into me imagining
   It could pierce my breast with them
   It would hurt me about as much as this
   Chap's words. Go to it!
   But many a man will pay me for these days
   For midst the games of whist and cans of ale
   The ink's not faded from the page on which

They wrote that I was Edward's whore and therefore
Banished.
Here comes my freshly painted king with a crowd
Of peers. I'll stand to one side.

He hides. Enter EDWARD, KENT, MORTIMER, ARCH-
BISHOP OF WINCHESTER, LANCASTER.

ARCHBISHOP:
　　My lord! Having read mass
　　Over the everlasting ashes of
　　Edward the First of England, your good father,
　　I bring this message to you:
　　Upon his deathbed he enjoined an oath—
LANCASTER:
　　When he'd grown whiter than his linen was—
ARCHBISHOP:
　　Upon your peers: Never again in England
　　Shall the man be seen.
GAVESTON (*hidden*):
　　Mort dieu!
ARCHBISHOP:
　　If you love us, my lord, hate Gaveston!

　　GAVESTON *whistles through his teeth.*

LANCASTER:
　　Let him cross the Irish sea and England
　　Will see cold steel.
EDWARD:
　　I will have Gaveston.
GAVESTON:
　　Well done, Eddie.
LANCASTER:
　　We're only saying: oaths aren't broken lightly.
ARCHBISHOP:
　　My lord, why do you stir your peers up so?
　　They really wished to love you and respect you.

EDWARD:

>   I will have Gaveston.

LANCASTER:

>   England could see so much cold steel,
>   my lords.

KENT:

>   If England sees cold steel, Lord Lancaster,
>   There will be heads, brother, to stick on poles
>   Because the tongues in them are far too long.

ARCHBISHOP:

>   *Our* heads!

EDWARD:

>   Yes, yours. That's why I hoped
>   That you'd back down.

LANCASTER:

>   Our heads are protected by our hands, I think.

>   *The* PEERS *leave.*

KENT:

>   Drop Gaveston. But check the peers, brother.

EDWARD:

>   Brother, I stand or fall with Gaveston.

GAVESTON (*comes forward*):

>   I can hold back no longer, my dear master.

EDWARD:

>   What, Danny! Dearest!
>   Embrace me, Danny, as I do you!
>   Since you were banished, all my days are barren.

GAVESTON:

>   And since I left, no soul in Hades suffered
>   More than poor Gaveston.

EDWARD:

>   I know. Now, mischief-making Lancaster,
>   Arch-heretic Winchester, plot all you want.
>   Gaveston, this very moment we will make you

Lord Chamberlain, Chancellor, Earl of Cornwall
And Peer of the Isle of Man.

KENT (*darkly*):

Brother, enough!

EDWARD:

Brother, be quiet!

GAVESTON:

My lord, don't crush me, what will people say?
Maybe that it's too much for a butcher's son.

EDWARD:

Afraid? You shall have bodyguards.
Need money? Go to my treasury.
Want to be feared? Here are my ring and seal.
Give orders in our name just as you please.

GAVESTON:

Your love has made me equal with the Caesars.

Enter the ABBOT OF COVENTRY.

EDWARD:

Where goes my lord the Abbot of Coventry?

ABBOT:

To attend your father's requiem, my lord.

EDWARD (*pointing to* GAVESTON):

My father has a guest from the Irish sea.

ABBOT:

What? Is the boy Gaveston back again?

GAVESTON:

He is, young fellow, and in London town
There's weeping and wailing and gnashing of teeth.

ABBOT:

I have done but what my oath obliged me to,
And if you're there again illegally
I'll bring your case to Parliament again
And back you'll go to Ireland, Gaveston.

GAVESTON (*seizing him*):

You come with me, there's water in the gutter,

And since you, Master Parson, wrote that statement,
I'll dip you, though an abbot, in the gutter,
Just as you dipped me in the Irish sea.

EDWARD:

It's good because you do it. What you do
Is good. Dip him in, Gaveston, and wash
His face. Barber your foe with gutter water!

KENT:

O brother, don't lay violent hands on him!
He'll make a protest at St. Peter's throne!

EDWARD:

Give him his life. Take his money and holdings.
You be the abbot. That one there is banished.

ABBOT:

God will get back at you, King Edward!

EDWARD:

But, before he does, run, Danny, get your hands
On all the Abbot's money and his lands!

GAVESTON:

What's a parson doing anyway with such a home?

*Mismanagement under King Edward's rule in the years
1307-1312. A war is lost in Scotland through the king's
negligence.*

London.

SPENCER, BALDOCK, *the* TWO PERSONS, SOLDIERS.

BALDOCK: The Archbishop of Winchester declared from
    the pulpit that there are worms in the grain this year.
    That means something.

SECOND: But not to us. The grain all goes to Winchester.

FIRST: Someone from Yorkshire has pawned the provisions
    for the Scotch troops.

BALDOCK: That's why the beer drinking at Eddie's started
    at eight in the morning.

SPENCER: Eddie passed out yesterday.

FIRST: How come?

SPENCER: The Earl of Cornwall told him he was growing a beard.   -

BALDOCK: On Tanner Street the other day, Eddie vomited.

SECOND: How come?

BALDOCK: A woman crossed his path.

SECOND: Heard the latest about the Earl of Cornwall? He's wearing a bustle.

Laughter.

A BALLAD PEDDLER *enters.*

BALLAD PEDDLER:
Eddie's concubine has hair on his chest
Pray for us, pray for us, pray for us
So the war in Scotland was laid to rest
Pray for us, pray for us, pray for us
There are far too many shillings in the pocket at Cornwall's rump
Pray for us, pray for us, pray for us
So Paddy has no arms left and O'Kelly has only a stump
Eddie is rolling his Gavy, which keeps him occupied
Pray for us, pray for us, pray for us
So Johnny got his in the rushes of the swamp at Bannockbride
Pray for us, pray for us, pray for us.

SPENCER:
The song is worth its ha'penny, my dear sir.

Enter EDWARD *and* GAVESTON.

EDWARD:
My Gaveston, you've only me for friend.
Leave them. We'll go to Tynemouth pond
Fishing and eating fish, riding and
Strolling on the redoubts knee to knee.

SPENCER (*grabbing the* BALLAD PEDDLER): That is high
     treason, sir. And if you tear my aunt's nephew to bits,
     my mother's son won't be able to stand it if anyone
     gets a little too personal about the dear Earl of Corn-
     wall.

GAVESTON: What are you after, my good friend?

SPENCER: I'm very partial to a pretty ditty, my lord, but
     high treason goes against the grain.

GAVESTON:
     Who was it?

SPENCER:
     This worm-eaten peg leg, my lord.

The BALLAD PEDDLER *makes himself scarce.*

GAVESTON (*to the king*):
     Calumniare audacter, semper aliquid haeret.*

SPENCER:
     You are saying the gallows are too good for him.

GAVESTON (*to* SPENCER):
     Follow me.

Off with the king. SPENCER *makes a sign to* BAL-
DOCK, *and they follow. Those who remain laugh.*

Enter ARCHBISHOP *and* LANCASTER.

ARCHBISHOP: London is laughing at us. The tenant farmers
     are asking how long the peers and Parliament can
     take it. In every street one hears the words *civil war*.

LANCASTER:
     A whore doesn't make war.

London.

MORTIMER, *in his house, among books, alone.*

---

* "Attack viciously, something will always strike," i.e., If
you sling enough mud, some of it will stick.—*E.B.*

MORTIMER:

    Plutarch relates of Caius Julius Caesar
    He read and wrote, dictated to his scribe
    And beat the Gauls, all in one breath. It seems
    That people of his ilk derived their fame
    From a strange lack of any insight into
    The nullity of human things and deeds
    And from a striking lack of seriousness.
    Their superficiality is amazing!

    Enter ARCHBISHOP *and* PEERS.

ARCHBISHOP:

    In your retreat you revel, Mortimer,
    In classic writings and in meditations
    On bygone times
    While like an ant heap in confusion London
    Needs you.

MORTIMER:

    London needs grain.

ARCHBISHOP:

    If for lack of grain the Lord above
    Lets a hundred swine die in St. James's Hospital
    We certainly won't take you from your books
    On that account, good Mortimer.
    But if one such swine wallows in Westminster
    Suckled with this land's milk by him who should
    Be guardian of this land, a king,
    Then certainly the time has come to let
    The classics just be classics.

MORTIMER:

    Classical authors say Great Alexander
    Loved his Hephaestion, Alcibiades
    Was loved by wise old Socrates, Achilles
    Pined for Patroclus. Shall I now
    For such a sport of nature show my face
    To the sweating people in the marketplace?

ARCHBISHOP:

> Yet Eddie's catapults—his long strong arms—
> By taking the top twelve inches off your body
> Could take the fun out of your hard-won leisure.
> Avoiding rain, you yet could drown in a flood.
> You're passionately cold and at the age
> When thought precedes action. You are schooled
> In sharp perception of human weakness, you're
> Experienced both in books and lively action,
> Great by descent, by property, by troops,
> And called to raise your voice in Westminster.

MORTIMER:

> You want to heat your soup in Etna's flames?
> You've come to the wrong man.
> Who starts to pluck a chicken
> Either to eat it or because its clucking
> Was such a nuisance
> When he's done the job
> May have acquired such an itch in his fingers that
> He's got to skin a tiger. Had you thought of that?

ARCHBISHOP:

> Though Westminster Hall come crashing to the ground
> We must get this peasant off our necks at once!

MORTIMER:

> My lords, as a solution I suggest
> We get this fellow's banishment signed and sealed.

ARCHBISHOP (*quickly*):

> And you can make that good in Parliament.
> In England's name we thank you, Mortimer,
> For sacrificing your pursuit of wisdom
> To England's welfare.

> ARCHBISHOP *and* PEERS *leave.*

MORTIMER (*alone*):

> Because a few hats are off and on the ground
> Before a son of a bitch, the English people
> Push their island over the precipice.

London.

MORTIMER, ARCHBISHOP, LANCASTER, *the two* PEERS.

LANCASTER:
> The King of England shows the Earl of Cornwall
> His catapults.

ARCHBISHOP:
> Shows *us* his catapults.

LANCASTER:
> Are you afraid, Archbishop?

MORTIMER:
> Alas, this shows our smallness, Lancaster.
> If the ancients had taken part in this our drama
> He'd have left the monarch's bosom long ago:
> The butcher's son would have swung from the com-
>   mon gallows,
> A little swollen with poison and without
> His teeth.

LANCASTER (*after a catapult has gone off*):
> Well aimed, Edward. Such shots give food for thought.
> For catapults are Edward's long strong arms.
> He strikes at your Scotch castles, Archbishop,
> With those things.

> *Enter* QUEEN ANNE.

MORTIMER:
> Where goes your majesty so fast?

ANNE:
> Deep in the woods, my noble Mortimer,
> There to dwell in grief and bitterness.
> My lord the king no longer sees me
> But only this man Gaveston.
> He hangs about his neck and if I come
> He wrinkles up his brow. "Oh, go away!
> Can you not see that I have Gaveston?"

MORTIMER:

>You're widowed by a butcher's son, my lady.

ARCHBISHOP:

>How Mortimer comforts my lady!

LANCASTER:

>She's devoted to bad Edward. What a fate!

ANNE:

>Good Mortimer, is there a bitterer thing
>Than that the French king's sister is a widow
>And not a widow, since her husband's living?
>Worse than a widow: it were better if
>The good earth covered her. Disgraced
>She walks in shadow, wife and not wife, for
>Her bed is empty.

MORTIMER:

>Too many tears are bad for the complexion,
>And orphan nights make you grow old, and rancid
>Feelings leave you limp. What you need, lady,
>Is satisfaction. Our rude
>Flesh in general needs lubrication.

ANNE (*to herself*):

>Miserable Edward, how low you've brought me
>That I can't strike this fellow in the face but
>Must hold my tongue and stand there when
>He leaps at me in lust.
>(*Aloud*):
>You exploit my misery, Mortimer.

MORTIMER:

>Turn back to court. And let these peers here worry.
>Before the moon changes, the butcher's son
>Shall be on an Irish boat.

ARCHBISHOP:

>Gaveston is a thorn in our eye, my lady:
>We'd pluck him out.

ANNE:

>But do not raise your swords against your king.
>Edward's estranged from us . . . Alas, my love

Confuses me . . .
How could I go off to the woods, my lords,
If you are going to fall upon King Edward?
On far-off roads I hear him threatened and
Come hurrying back to help him in his need.

LANCASTER:
Gaveston won't leave England without bloodshed.

ANNE:
Then let him stay.
Rather than my lord's life
Should be menaced,
I'll learn to bear my life
And leave him
Gaveston.

LANCASTER:
Be patient, lady.

MORTIMER:
My lords, let's accompany the Queen
Back to Westminster.

ANNE:
For my sake do not raise your swords against
The king.

All leave.

Enter GAVESTON.

GAVESTON:
It looks as if the Earl of Lancaster,
The Archbishop of Winchester, the Queen,
And several vultures from the city of London
Are hatching a plot against a number of people.

London.

GAVESTON, *in his house, alone, writing his will.*

GAVESTON:
By a misunderstanding, on an ordinary Thursday,

Also without any liking for slaughter,
Many a man is wiped out, painfully.
And therefore I
Who do not know
What it was about me of too much or too little
That made this Edward, now the king,
Unable to leave me alone,
For my own mother found nothing in me
Any different from the extremely
Usual, no goiter, no white skin,
Therefore I
Who have come to the end of my rope
But do know (stupid as I am)
That nothing helps him live whom all wish dead
So there's no help for me here in London
And I won't get out of the place except feet first
Therefore I
Write my last will and testament.
I, Danyell Gaveston, twenty-seven years old,
Son of a butcher, finished
By overfavorable circumstances and erased
By too much luck bequeath
Clothing and boots to those
Who were around when I died.
To the dumb women of St. James Street
The Abbey of Coventry. To the good
Ale-swilling English people my narrow grave.
To the good King Edward, my friend,
God's forgiveness.
For it troubles me that I did not simply
Turn to dust.

*9 May 1311: Since King Edward refuses to sign his name
to the banishment of his favorite Gaveston, a thirteen-year
war breaks out.*

Westminster.

MORTIMER, LANCASTER, ARCHBISHOP, PEERS *are signing a document, one after the other.*

MORTIMER:
> This parchment sets the seal on his banishment.

> *Enter* QUEEN, GAVESTON, *who sits down next to the king's chair,* KENT, *then* EDWARD.

EDWARD:
> You're angry because Gaveston sits here?
> It is our wish. We want to have it so.

LANCASTER:
> Your grace does well to place him at your side.
> Nowhere else would the new peer be so safe.

ARCHBISHOP:
> Quam male conveniunt!*

LANCASTER:
> A lion that flatters his own lice!

FIRST PEER:
> Look how the fellow lolls upon his chair!

SECOND PEER:
> The people of London will have the time of their lives
> Seeing King Edward thus—with both his wives.

The Parliament is opened to the public.

KENT:
> Roger Mortimer has the floor.

---

* "How badly matched!" In Marlowe, the phrase is a word to the wise, who knew it went on in the original: "How badly matched . . . are Majesty and Love." (Ovid, *Metamorphoses*, II. 846.) Jove, Ovid says, had to become a bull to seduce Europa: Brecht picks up this image later (see p. 79), applying it to Mortimer and the Queen.—*E.B.*

MORTIMER:

When Paris ate King Menelaus' bread
And salt in Menelaus' house, the wife
Of Menelaus slept with him—that's what
The ancient chronicles report—and lay
Upon his hempen bunk as he sailed for Troy.
Troy laughed. And it seemed only fair to laughing
Troy—Greece thought so too—to give this willing
Flesh by the name of Helen back to her
Greek husband, for she was a whore. Only
Paris beat about the bush, understandably,
And said she wasn't well. Meanwhile ships came,
Greek ships. Ships multiplied like fleas. One morning
Greeks forced their way in Paris' house to remove
The Greek whore from it. Paris yelled from the
    window
This was *his* house, this was *his* city, and
The Trojans, thinking he wasn't wrong, applauded
With a grin.
The Greeks stretch out on the sails that they have
    furled
And fish. Till in an alehouse by the dockside
A man socks another man, gives him a bloody nose,
His pretext being it was for Helen's sake.
Quite unexpectedly on the following days
The hands of many reached for many throats.
From the beat-up ships they harpooned the drowning
Like tuna fish. As the moon waxed,
Many were missing from the tents, and in the houses
Many were found, headless. In the Skamander
The crabs grew fat in those years: but no one ate
    them.
On the lookout for stormy weather in the morning
Worried only whether the fish would bite in the
    evening
Toward noon bewildered and willing, they

All fell.
Seen at ten o'clock
They still had faces.
Toward eleven forgetting their native speech
The Trojan sees Troy, the Greek sees Greece, no
    more:
They see instead the metamorphosis
Of human lips into the fangs of tigers.
Toward noon teeth hit the flanks of the fellow-beast
Which sets up a groan.
Yet were there one man on the beleaguered wall
Who knew and called them by their names
According to their kind
Many would stop in their tracks and freeze.
It would be good if they would simply vanish
Fighting, fighting, on suddenly aging ships,
Sinking underfoot before nightfall,
Nameless!
More frightfully they kill each other.
As that war dragged on ten years
And is named Trojan
And was ended by
A horse.
If then the human, inhuman ear of reason
Had not for the most part been stopped up
—No matter whether Helen was a whore
Or had a score of healthy grandchildren—
Troy, four times larger than this London,
Would still be standing
Hector, his genitals bleeding,
Would not have been destroyed
The ancient hair of weeping Priam
Would not have been spat on by sons of bitches
And this whole race of men
Would not have died out
In the noontide of its day.

Quod erat demonstrandum. It's true that in that case
We wouldn't have had
The Iliad.

He sits. Pause.

EDWARD *weeps.*

ANNE:
What ails you, husband? Do you want some water?
KENT:
The king's not well. We'll meet now in closed session!

The Parliament now meets in closed session.

EDWARD:
What are you looking at? Don't look. God grant
Your tongue is not a liar's, Mortimer.
Don't worry about me. If it looks as if
I were out of sorts, forget it. It's just
Discolored temples, a stoppage of blood in the brain,
That's all.
Lay hands on the traitor Mortimer!
ARCHBISHOP:
What he says here we'll answer with our heads.
LANCASTER:
Remove Gaveston from our sight, my lord.
MORTIMER:
Read here what we have written on this parchment.
ANNE (*to* EDWARD):
Try to understand, sir. It's Thursday, it's London.
MORTIMER:
Sign
The banishment of Danyell Gaveston, son
Of a butcher in the city of London,
Banished long years ago by the English Parliament,
Illegally returned, today banished for the second time
By the English Parliament. Sir! Sign!

LANCASTER:

Pray sign, my lord!

ARCHBISHOP:

My lord, pray sign!

GAVESTON:

You could hardly have believed it would go this fast.

KENT:

Drop Gaveston, brother Edward.

MORTIMER:

It's Thursday. It's London. Sign!

LANCASTER, ARCHBISHOP, PEERS *place a table before the king.*

Sign!

EDWARD:

Never, never, never! Before I let
Gaveston be taken from me, I'll leave the island.

ARCHBISHOP:

England is torn in two.

LANCASTER:

Much blood will flow in England now, King Edward.

MORTIMER (*singing*):

The English girls wore black and cried
When their lovers died at Bannockbride
Aheave and aho!
The English king ordered his drummer boys
To drown out the Bannockbride widows' noise
With Arom Rombelow.

EDWARD:

Won't you go on singing? You look a king over
Like an ox in your stockyards, don't you?
Can a race of men live like that?
Come, Gaveston. I am still there and my feet
Know what to do with vipers.

Off, with GAVESTON.

MORTIMER:

    So it's war.

LANCASTER:

    Nor devils of the ocean nor angels of the sky
    Can save him from our army. The butcher's son
       must die.

The battle of Killingworth, 15 and 16 August 1320.

Battlefield near Killingworth.

Toward seven in the evening.

MORTIMER, LANCASTER, ARCHBISHOP, TROOPS.

LANCASTER:

    Behold the tattered banner of St. George
    As it has waved from Ireland all the way
    To the Dead Sea. Sound the alarm!

    Enter KENT.

KENT:

    My lords, my love for England drives me to
    Your banner. I renounce the king, my brother,
    For his accursed attachment to this Gaveston
    Is ruining the realm.

ARCHBISHOP:

    Your hand on it.

LANCASTER:

    March!

    Drums.

    And let none touch King Edward!

ARCHBISHOP:

    A hundred shillings on the head of Gaveston!

    They march.

Toward seven in the evening. Marching men.

EDWARD, GAVESTON, TROOPS.

FIRST SOLDIER:
  Come, my lord, come, the battle has begun.
EDWARD:
  Speak on, Gaveston.
GAVESTON:
  Many in London said the war would never end.
EDWARD:
  Our eye is most particularly moved
  To see you, Gaveston, stand before us
  At such a time, unarmed, trusting us,
  Protected nor by leather nor by bronze,
  Mere naked skin within the accustomed Irish suit!
SECOND SOLDIER:
  Give the order to march, my lord,
  The battle's begun.
EDWARD:
  Like the triangle
  Formed by that flock of storks in the sky,
  Which seems to stand, though flying,
  So stands your image in our heart
  Undimmed by time.
GAVESTON:
  My lord, such simple arithmetic as
  A fisherman does before he goes to sleep
  Counting nets and fish, and totting up
  The day's earnings
  I won't omit to do, even walking in the sun.
  Many are more than one.
  Such a one lives many days but not all days.
  So do not set too high a stake on your heart
  For fear your heart be forfeit.
THIRD SOLDIER:
  Sir! Into battle!

EDWARD:
>   Your beautiful hair.

Eight in the evening.

GAVESTON (*fleeing*):
>   Since these drums started
>   And the swamp's been sucking up
>   Horses and catapults
>   My mother's son has been going crazy.
>   Stop panting, Gaveston! I wonder
>   If everyone is drowned and done for and
>   Nothing left but noise suspended
>   Between earth and sky?
>   I'm not going to run any more either; for
>   It's only a matter of minutes and
>   I've no one's hand to touch, I'll simply
>   Lie down there on the ground and not try
>   To live to the end of time. And if
>   King Edward should ride by tomorrow to torture me
>   And if he should shout: "Danyell, where are you?"
>   I won't be there. So
>   Tie your shoelaces, Gav, and sit
>   Tight.

>   *Enter* LANCASTER, MORTIMER, ARCHBISHOP, PEERS,
>   TROOPS.

LANCASTER:
>   At him, men!

>   *Laughter from the* PEERS.

>   Welcome, Lord Chamberlain!
FIRST PEER:
>   Welcome, beloved Earl of Cornwall!

ARCHBISHOP:

Welcome, Abbot!

LANCASTER:

Running around to cool your filthy blood?

ARCHBISHOP:

Most worthy peers, the trial can be brief.
The verdict: Since this Danyell Gaveston
Son of a butcher in the city of London
Was King Edward's whore
And led him into vice and crime, and even
Twofold exile did not keep him from it
He'll be hanged from a tree.
Hang him!

JAMES:

My lords,
He's motionless, stiff as a frozen codfish.
We'll use that branch. Two hempen ropes. He's over-
weight.

MORTIMER (*to one side*):

Alive, this chap would be worth the half of Scotland.
A man like me could give the whole army
For this watery codfish. But
Branch, rope, and neck are there and blood is cheap.
Since catapults with men attached
Stomp irresistibly on
Since hordes of horses with people on them
Scared of the drumming
Rush madly at each other, and
Walls of dust and the onset of night seal up
All the exits from the battle,
Since catapults labor and drums drum and
Manned hordes of horses eat each other up
The red and giddy moon draws reason out of brains,
And out of man
Naked
Steps the beast.

The situation demands that now
Someone be hanged.

JAMES:
Now that plank.

GAVESTON:
The rope isn't right.

JAMES:
We'll soap it right away.

SOLDIERS (*singing in the background*):
Eddie's concubine has hair on his chest
Pray for us, pray for us, pray for us.

A SOLDIER (*to* GAVESTON):
How are you feeling, sir?

GAVESTON:
First stop the drum.

SOLDIER:
Are you going to scream, sir?

GAVESTON:
Please take the drum away. I shall not scream.

JAMES:
Right, sir, now shut your trap.
Put the noose on. He has a short neck.

GAVESTON:
One thing I beg: let it happen fast.
But first I also beg you read the verdict.

JAMES (*reads the verdict; then*):
All right: now!

GAVESTON:
Edward! My friend Edward! Help me
If you're still in this world! Edward!

Enter a SOLDIER.

SOLDIER:
Stop. A message from the king!

GAVESTON:
He *is* still in this world.

ARCHBISHOP (*reading*):

>"Since I have learned you've taken Gaveston
>I request permission to see him before he dies
>For I know he will die.
>I send my word and seal he will come back.
>If you should wish to do me, lords, this favor
>I should be grateful for the courtesy:
>Edward."

GAVESTON:

>Edward!

ARCHBISHOP:

>What now?

LANCASTER:

>This piece of paper stands in the scale against
>A battle won.

GAVESTON:

>Edward. The name revives me.

LANCASTER:

>It needn't. We could, for example,
>Send the king your heart.

GAVESTON:

>You have the promise of our good King Edward
>And that with word and seal:
>He'll only see me and then send me back.

LANCASTER:

>When?

Laughter.

>For his Danny's sake, if he catches a glimpse of him,
>He'll break the seal under God's very nose.

ARCHBISHOP:

>Ere English king break oath let this whole island
>Break to bits and fall into the ocean!

LANCASTER:

>Good. Send him Gaveston but hang him first.

MORTIMER:

>Do not hang Gaveston but do not send him either.

ARCHBISHOP:

>The king's wish must be executed but
>So, maybe, must the king's friend.

LANCASTER:

>Skin him, you'd say, but don't refuse him
>Any small courtesy. Very well.
>Now let's do battle with this Edward Gloster
>Wife of the butcher's son.

ARCHBISHOP:

>Cut him loose.
>And you, Lord Mortimer, take charge of him.

GAVESTON:

>One watch of the night to go, two paths to tread.
>My death I carry with me like my moon.

JAMES:

>Much fuss about a simple butcher's son!

All, off; except MORTIMER, JAMES, GAVESTON.

MORTIMER:

>He's the alpha of the war, this butcher's son,
>Its omega too, and if I manage
>To do the right thing at the right time, then
>I have him.
>Hullo! James!
>Take this man and when they ask you: where
>Are you taking this man?
>Say: to the carrion pit. But
>Handle him like a raw egg. And bring him
>Tomorrow, toward eleven o'clock, into the Killing-
>>worth woods
>Where I shall be.

JAMES:

>But if anything happens to you, my lord?

MORTIMER:

>Do as you like.

JAMES:

>Come, sir.

Off, with GAVESTON.

MORTIMER:
My instructions, or so I feel, give off a faint
Odor of carrion.
The moon sucks blood like mist and all these peers
Have faces that smack of death, while I
Who know what's what and pay no heed to moons,
Am just a lump of cowardice.
One man suffices to dispatch him who could
Dispatch a thousand.
So, frightened like one burned to death,
I wrap myself in the skin of another man:
This butcher's son.

Toward ten at night.

ANNE (*alone*):
Oh, most unhappy Queen!
Oh, how I wish that when I left fair France
The waters of the Channel had turned to stone!
Or that those arms that hung about my neck
Had strangled me on my wedding night!
Alas, that now I must pursue King Edward
Since, widowing me, he will do battle
For the devil Gaveston at Killingworth.
I tremble from head to foot to look at Edward
But he makes a sponge of his heart and soaks it
In *him*
And so I am forever miserable.
O God, why hast Thou put down Anne of France
Only to raise the devil Gaveston?

Enter GAVESTON, JAMES, SOLDIER.

JAMES (*coming forward*):
Ho, there.

ANNE:

Soldiers of King Edward?

JAMES:

By no means.

ANNE:

Who is that man there in the Irish dress?

JAMES:

Danyell Gaveston: whore of the King of England.

ANNE:

Where are you taking him?

JAMES:

To the carrion pit.

GAVESTON (*at the back*):

If only I had water for my feet.

SOLDIER:

There's water.

ANNE:

I beg you: don't refuse it to him.

GAVESTON:

Let me go to her, it is the Queen.

Take me with you, my lady.

JAMES:

No, stay. But wash your feet, I have permission for
        that.

ANNE:

Why don't you let him speak with me?

JAMES:

Go to one side, your grace, while he washes himself.

He urges her to go.

GAVESTON:

Stay, my dear lady, stay!

Miserable Gaveston, where are you going now?

One o'clock in the morning.

LANCASTER, PEERS, TROOPS, *on the march toward Boroughbridge.*

A SOLDIER:
    The way to Boroughbridge.

    The password is handed along.

SOLDIERS (*singing*):
    The English girls wore black and cried
    In the night
    When their lovers died at Bannockbride
    In the night
    Cried: Aheave and aho!
    The English king ordered his drummer boys
    In the night
    To drown out the Bannockbride widows' noise
    In the night
    With Arom Rombelow.

LANCASTER:
    All goes well. We'll take Boroughbridge tonight.

Two o'clock in the morning.

EDWARD, SPENCER, BALDOCK, YOUNG EDWARD, *the sleeping army.*

EDWARD:
    I'm longing for an answer from the peers
    About my friend, my Gaveston. O Spencer,
    Not all the gold in England were enough
    To ransom him. He's doomed to die. I know
    Mortimer's evil nature. And I know
    The Archbishop is ungentle and Lancaster's
    Relentless and I'll never see again
    Danyell Gaveston, and in the end
    They'll set their foot on my neck.

SPENCER:

Were I King Edward, Sovereign in England,
Heir to great Edward Longshanks, I'd not bear
These raging rowdies, I would not permit
These tramps of peers to threaten me in my
Own land. Strike off their heads! Stick them on poles!
It always works, that method.

EDWARD:

You're right, good Spencer, we were much too mild,
Too nice with them. It's time to stop.
Should Gaveston not come, their heads will fly!

BALDOCK:

You owe it to yourself, a plan like that.

YOUNG EDWARD:

Why are they making such a noise, father?

EDWARD:

They're tearing England apart, my child.
I should have sent you to them, Edward,
To make them do my will with Gaveston.
Would you have been afraid, young man,
Before all those wild peers?

YOUNG EDWARD:

Yes, father.

EDWARD:

That's a good answer.
There are many evil birds on the field tonight.

Enter the QUEEN.

ANNE:

Are you King Edward's men?
Is that Killingworth quarry?
Where is King Edward, soldiers?

SPENCER:

What's this?

A SOLDIER:

A woman looking for King Edward.

ANNE:

Coming from London, two whole days on horseback,
I've sought you out through battle, thicket, swamp.

EDWARD:

You are not welcome.

SPENCER:

For two whole days the battle's been in labor
The more so since one army's like the other
And both sides cry: For England and St. George!
Brother tears brother's flesh crying: St. George!
Army bites into army like a pair
Of salamanders intertwined in struggle.
England's villages burn in England's name.
Toward evening, in the swamp, among drowning
Catapults, where Gaveston was taken,
Report would have it Lord Arundel fell.
Then rain came down. A sound of skirmishing
Rent the night air. The king was cold but not
Downhearted. Our position is not bad
Unless the peers have taken Boroughbridge
During the night. Today's decisive. For Gaveston
The peers have promised to send him to us.

ANNE (*to herself*):

And to drag him to the carrion pit.
Maybe that's best. But not for me to tell him
The man must be in the next world already.
(*Aloud:*)
Today you are the hunted, Edward.

EDWARD:

Yes. And my friend Gaveston is taken,
And through the swamp and shrubbery *you've* come.

ANNE:

If you want to spit on me, here's my face.

EDWARD:

Your face is a gravestone. On it's written:
"Here lies poor Gaveston."
Have you no word of comfort for me? Like:

"Be comforted, my lord, this Gaveston
Squinted in one eye." To which I answer:
"All human flesh repels me: yours for instance."
I, Edward of England, mindful that maybe
Only hours stand between me and my fall
Can tell you this: I do not like you.
In the hour of death: I still love Gaveston.

ANNE:

Though I shall not forget this hard insult—
For the little I have in my head stays there
And fades away but slowly—
It's just as well that fellow is not here.

EDWARD:

Get him back to me.
They say that Mortimer has all the power.
Go to him, he's vain enough. His type's
Susceptible to Queens.
Go at him, use your skills, your special ones.
The world's
About to come to an end in any case.
And what's an oath? I give you absolution.

ANNE:

O Christ in Heaven! I cannot.

EDWARD:

Thus do I banish you my sight!

ANNE:

In these days when a war is starting which,
So they say, will never end, d'you send me
Back through this horde of raging butchers?

EDWARD:

Yes. And I also commission you to
Fetch troops from Scotland for your son, young
    Edward.
His father's cause is in bad shape, you know.

ANNE:

O cruel Edward!

EDWARD:

> This too I tell you, it's your fate:
> You're tied to this no doubt cruel Edward who
> Knows you from your heart to your vagina
> Until you die like the trapped beast in the snare.

ANNE:

> Are you sure this bond's inviolable?

EDWARD:

> You are my property. I have title to you,
> A thing assigned to me, unasked for,
> And never to be free till I consent!

ANNE:

> You send me away and bind me, both at once?

EDWARD:

> Yes.

ANNE:

> Heaven is my witness that I love but you.
> I thought my arms, to hold you, stretched over all
> The island.
> It is to be feared that you grow tired.
> You bind and send me away now, both at once?

EDWARD:

> Is there still no news of Gaveston?

ANNE:

> Who bids me go and does not let me go
> All men shall go from him and not let him go.
> Sleepless, skinless,
> May he pray for his death and not get it!
> When he'd take a fellow creature by the hand
> May the skin be skinned off from that hand
> By leprosy!
> And when he'd run from men to die
> May they stop him in his tracks and
> Not let him go!

EDWARD:

> Is there still no news of Gaveston?

ANNE:

>If you're still waiting for your friend, King Edward,
>Cut short that hope. In the swamp
>I saw a man in Irish dress. I heard them say
>He was on his way to the carrion pit.

SPENCER:

>Oh, bloody perjury!

EDWARD (*kneeling*):

>By all your mothers and by mother earth
>By Heaven and by the great plains of the stars
>By this hard and dried-up hand
>By all the steel on this island
>By the last oaths of an unburdened breast
>By every English honor, by my teeth:
>I'll have your miscreated bodies and I'll change them
>Till your mothers do not know you!
>I'll have your white and headless stumps!

ANNE:

>I see it now. Edward, body and soul,
>Has sold himself to the devil Gaveston.

>*Off, with* YOUNG EDWARD. *Enter a* SOLDIER.

SOLDIER:

>The peers answer:
>"We've taken Boroughbridge. The battle's done.
>If you want relief and help without bloodshed
>England advises: Forget Gaveston
>Who is not in the quarrel any more—"

EDWARD:

>Who is not in the world any more—

SOLDIER:

>"Renounce his memory and peace is yours."

EDWARD:

>Good. Tell your peers:
>Because you've taken Boroughbridge and I therefore
>Cannot do battle now and because
>My good friend Gaveston's not of this world

I accept your offer.
Let there be peace between us.
Come toward noon into the limestone quarry
At Killingworth where I, as you requested,
Will renounce his memory.
But come without weapons for they would offend
Our kingly eye.

SOLDIER *off.*

EDWARD (*wakes his own soldiers*):
Up, slugabeds! Into the quarry with you!
Quiet as corpses now!
Edward of the Gentle Hand's expecting guests.
When they arrive,
Hurl yourselves at their throats!

Five o'clock in the morning.

GAVESTON, JAMES, *the* OTHER SOLDIER.

GAVESTON: Hell, where are we going? This is the quarry
again, we're moving in a circle. Why these cold
looks? Fifty silver shillings! Five hundred! I don't
want to die!

Throws himself on the ground.

JAMES:
All right. Now you have screamed, we can go on.

Enter TWO SOLDIERS.

A CRY:
St. George and England!
FIRST SOLDIER:
What do you see?
SECOND SOLDIER:
Fire.

FIRST SOLDIER:

    It's Boroughbridge. What do you hear?

SECOND SOLDIER:

    Bells ringing.

FIRST SOLDIER: It's the bell-ropes of Bristol, and they're
    pulling them because the King of England and his
    peers want to make peace.

SECOND SOLDIER:

    Why, all at once?

FIRST SOLDIER:

    Supposedly so England won't be torn limb from limb.

JAMES: It looks now as if you may get off with nothing
    worse than a black eye, good sir. What time is it?

OTHER SOLDIER:

    Toward five o'clock.

Eleven in the morning.

EDWARD, SPENCER, BALDOCK.

SPENCER:

    The peers of England are coming, unarmed, from
       the hills.

EDWARD:

    Are the guards on duty?

SPENCER:

    Yes.

EDWARD:

    D'you all have ropes?

SPENCER:

    Yes.

EDWARD:

    Are the troops all set to fall on the headless army?

SPENCER:

    Yes.

Enter ARCHBISHOP, LANCASTER, PEERS.

BALDOCK:
My lord, your peers!
EDWARD:
Tie them up with ropes!
PEERS (*roaring*):
Treachery! We've fallen into a trap. Your oath!
EDWARD:
Perjury thrives in weather like this.
ARCHBISHOP:
You swore!
EDWARD:
My drums!

*The drums drown out the cries of the peers. The
PEERS are led off, tied up.*

SPENCER:
Mortimer is lacking.
EDWARD:
Fetch him.
Have you got crossbowmen, catapultmen, missile-
throwers?
Bring me maps!
Let our steel reach out over the plain!
Comb every inch of it!
Tell every man before you strangle him in the under-
growth
That England's king turned tiger
In the woods at Killingworth.
Forward!

A great battle.

Twelve noon.

GAVESTON, JAMES, *the* OTHER SOLDIER.

JAMES:

Dig, my lad. The battle grows. Your friend will win.

GAVESTON:

Why do you need a hole?

JAMES: It's getting to be time to bring us in out of the
cold. We must carry out instructions, you see. Dig,
dear sir. If you want to pass water, sir, you can do
so here.

GAVESTON: The battle's moving over toward Bristol. When
the wind blows, you can hear the Welshmen's horses.
Have you read about the Trojan War? My mother's
son: for him, too, much blood was shed. Eddie may
be asking quite often where his friend is.

JAMES: I doubt it. Everyone in Killingworth will tell him
he needn't wait for you any more. Dig, dear sir. The
rumor's around, you see, that your honorable Irish
corpse has been seen in the Killingworth carrion pit.
If a rumor is ever to be believed, you have no head
now, sir.

GAVESTON:

Who's this pit for?

JAMES *is silent.*

Won't I see the king again, James?

JAMES:

The King of Heaven maybe. Hardly the King of
England.

OTHER SOLDIER:

Many have fallen today by a soldier's hand.

JAMES:

What time is it?

OTHER SOLDIER:

Toward twelve.

Seven in the evening.

EDWARD, SPENCER, BALDOCK, *the captured* PEERS, MORTI-
MER *among them.* SPENCER *is counting the captives and
noting down their names.*

EDWARD:
    The time has come.
    This is the hour
    That the murder of my friend
    Upon whom as is known my soul depended
    That the murder of my Gaveston shall be
    Atoned for.
KENT:
    Fate favored you and England, brother.
EDWARD (*setting him free*):
    There, sir. You have spoken. You may go.

    KENT *leaves.*

    Presumptuous peers, it isn't only luck:
    Sometimes the good cause wins the battle.
    You hang your heads, it seems, but we
    Will lift them up again for you.
    Scoundrels! Rebels! Accursed villains!
    Did you slaughter him?
    When we sent messengers to request
    (And gave our word and seal)
    That he come and see us, nothing more,
    Did you say Yes? Huh?
    Did you slaughter him? Behead him?
    You have a big head, Winchester.
    It towers over all the others now just as
    Your rage towered over all the others' rage.
ARCHBISHOP:
    And when I look into your perjured face
    I give up hope of reaching you with words.
    A man like you hardly believes the tongue

That sets him free from death, speaking pure truth.
There's no such thing as proof: you have effaced it.
The tie that binds us, you, your friend you've tangled:
Eternity won't disentangle it.
What you determine has a short term, Edward.

EDWARD:
And what do *you* know, Lancaster?

LANCASTER:
The worst is death, and death is better
Than to live with you in such a world.

MORTIMER (*to himself*):
Yet with me
Who am their butcher more than Edward now
They'd go together into a willing grave
And rot.

EDWARD:
Away with them! Off with their heads!

LANCASTER:
Farewell, time!
The day before yesterday
When in the evening the thin moon rose up high
God was still with us. And now
Although the moon that rises is not a great deal
        thicker
All is over.
Farewell, my Mortimer!

ARCHBISHOP:
My Mortimer, farewell!

MORTIMER:
Who loves his fatherland like us dies easy.
England mourns us. England will not forget.

ARCHBISHOP, LANCASTER, PEERS, *except* MORTIMER,
are led off.

EDWARD:
Has a certain Mortimer been found

Who when I gave the order in the quarry
At Killingworth was slyly lacking?

SPENCER:

Surely, my lord, here he is.

EDWARD:

Dispatch the others.
As for this man, who is not for forgetting,
Our Majesty has something else in mind.
Untie him: so the memory of this day
At Killingworth shall not be lost in England.
Dull-eyed, you Mortimers do arithmetic, and
Burrow in books, like worms.
But in books there is nothing about Edward who
Reads nothing, does not do arithmetic,
Knows nothing, and has intimate ties with Nature:
He's nourished by quite different food.
You may go, Lord Mortimer. Walk around
And, wandering, bear witness in the sun
How Edward Longshanks' son avenged his friend.

MORTIMER:

As for your friend, this Danyell Gaveston,
Toward five o'clock when England's king turned tiger,
He ran into the woods at Killingworth.
Yes, still alive.
And when my friends began to talk, had you
Not drowned their words out with your drums
Had not, that is, too little confidence
And too much passion, too swift anger
Troubled your eye, your favorite Gaveston
Would be still alive.

Exit.

EDWARD:

Against the hour when the corpse is found
Prepare a worthy grave. But do
Not hunt for him.
He's like the man who walks into the woods

And the bushes grow up thick behind him and
The plants shoot up again and
The thicket's got him.
But we would like to wipe this day's sweat off
Our bodies, eat and sleep it off, until
A cleansing of the realm from every vestige
Of fratricidal strife commands our services.
I won't set out for London again or sleep
In any but a soldier's hempen bed
Till this whole breed of men is swallowed up
In me like a drop of rain in the ocean.
Come, Spencer.

Three o'clock in the morning. Gentle wind.

ANNE (*alone*):
Since Edward of England, not hearing either prayer
Or urgent appeal, drove me to Mortimer
The cold of heart, I'll put on widow's weeds.
Four times I let my hair be spat upon
By him, and I preferred to stand bareheaded
Beneath the sky, not veiled as now.
But the fifth time, the wind is otherwise
The sky is of another sort
The breath from my lips is different.
To London!

MORTIMER *has entered.*

MORTIMER:
No, no, my lady, London brews watery soup
For such as we.
ANNE:
Where is your army, Mortimer?
MORTIMER:
My army lies dead between willows and quarry
And a nauseous swamp has swallowed very many
A mother's son. Where is your husband, lady?

ANNE:

With the dead Gaveston.

MORTIMER:

And the king of France's sister?

ANNE:

At the crossroads between England and Scotland.
He commissioned me to bring him troops from Scotland
On Killingworth day.

MORTIMER:

He commissioned me
To roam abroad, a living witness
To Killingworth day.
He struck off seven heads of the hydra:
May he find seven times seven when he wakes!
Trapped in his camp, trapped in his armies, he
Cannot pull free from the war or from the exterminated
Gaveston—

ANNE:

Who slighted his wife before everyone—

MORTIMER:

Who bled his realm white like a procurer—

ANNE:

Who held me captive and yet threw me away—

MORTIMER:

Who disemboweled the land like a shot deer—

ANNE:

Strike him down, Mortimer!

MORTIMER:

Because he kicked you aside like a scurvy bitch—

ANNE:

Because like a vicious bitch he kicked me aside—

MORTIMER:

You who were a queen—

ANNE:

I who was a child in innocence

Not knowing the world or mankind—

MORTIMER:
Sink your teeth in him!

ANNE:
I'd like to be a she-wolf
Hurtling through the bushes with teeth bared
And not rest
Till earth covers Edward Gloster who
Long ago lost his soul and the day before yesterday
      was
My husband:

She throws three handfuls of earth over her shoulder.

Whipping up the poor forest dwellers,
Stained with the cunning of bad worlds, bad men,
Roaming like a she-wolf and attacked by wolves,
Drenched by the rain of banishment,
Hardened by foreign wind—

MORTIMER:
Heap earth on Edward of England!

ANNE:
Heap earth upon Edward Gloster!

MORTIMER:
Now: to Scotland!

ANNE:
Woe to us, Mortimer! There now shall be
A war that hurls this island in the sea!

*After four years of war, King Edward finds himself still
in the field. Landing of Queen Anne. Harwich: 23 Sep-
tember 1324.*

A camp near Harwich.

EDWARD, SPENCER, BALDOCK.

EDWARD:
> Thus
> After four years of war and many betrayals
> Edward of England triumphed with his friends.

Enter a MESSENGER. *Hands over a message.*

SPENCER:
> Have you any news, my lord?

EDWARD (*tearing up the message*):
> No. Have you?

SPENCER:
> No.

EDWARD:
> How's that? I'd heard of a great battle and
> A thorough cleansing of the realm.

BALDOCK:
> All that, if I'm not mistaken, took place some
> Four years ago, my lord

EDWARD:
> Four splendid years.
> For life in tents, life in the train of armies,
> Tastes very good. Horses are very good.
> Wind cleans your lungs. And if your skin shrinks up
> And your hair falls out, the rain washes your kidneys
> And everything is so much better than in London.

BALDOCK:
> I prefer to curse at London *in* London.

EDWARD:
> Have you got that list?

SPENCER:
> For sure, my lord.

EDWARD:
> Let's hear it, please. Read it, Spencer.

SPENCER *reads out the list of executed peers.*

It seems one name is missing: Mortimer.

Have you offered a reward for the man who brings
    him in?

SPENCER:

We have, lord, and renewed it year by year.

EDWARD:

If he turns up in England, he'd be brought in fast.

Enter SECOND MESSENGER.

SECOND MESSENGER:

Rumor reports ship upon ship in the north.

EDWARD:

That means nothing. They are herring fishermen.
They live in the north.

SECOND MESSENGER *leaves.*

As for the others on that list
They were still barking several years ago.
Now they've stopped barking!
Now they do not bite!

BALDOCK (*to* SPENCER):

He believes nothing. Since he went into decline
He takes care to forget whatever's told him.

EDWARD:

Only where are those Scotch troops?
You're always hearing of troops. All false alarms!
And no news of the Scottish troops which years
Ago we sent the Queen for!

Enter the army.

FIRST SOLDIER:

The royal army, tried in four years' campaigning,
In which we slew so many peers like rats,
Now, lacking food, as well as shoes and clothes,
Asks the king, Edward, son of Edward Longshanks,
Father of England's army, for permission
To eat again the eels that swim in the Thames.

SOLDIERS:
> Long live King Edward!

SECOND SOLDIER:
> Our wives want children. It's just that the war
> Maybe won't ever end because King Edward
> Has sworn he won't sleep in a bed again
> Before he's brought the enemy to heel.

FIRST SOLDIER:
> And after so many have gone home declaring
> It was because of wills, or pregnant wives,
> Or liquor franchise, it'd be good to know
> If the king intends to go to London or not.

THIRD SOLDIER:
> Are you going to London, sir?

FOURTH SOLDIER:
> Or what *does* he intend?

EDWARD:
> To wage war against the cranes in the air
> The fish in the ocean, multiplying
> Quicker than you can kill them,
> Monday against the great Leviathan
> Thursday against the vultures of Wales.
> And now: I'll eat.

SPENCER:
> The watery food has made the king a little
> Delirious. Go.

SPENCER *and* BALDOCK *drive the soldiers out.*

EDWARD:
> Bring me something to drink, Baldock.

BALDOCK *leaves.*

SPENCER:
> They won't return.
> Won't you really go to London, lord?

Enter THIRD MESSENGER.

THIRD MESSENGER:

> My lord, at Harwich there are armed men in the
> forest.

EDWARD:

> Let them be. They work for the Welsh merchants.

He sits down to eat.

> Have any ships been sighted?

THIRD MESSENGER:

> Yes, lord.

EDWARD:

> Are villages burning in the north?

THIRD MESSENGER:

> Yes, lord.

EDWARD:

> That's the Queen on her way here with Scotch troops.

SPENCER:

> Hardly.

EDWARD:

> I don't like being looked at when I eat!

SPENCER *and* THIRD MESSENGER *leave.*

(*Alone:*)
It makes my blood boil that my son Edward
Could be seduced into supporting *them!*

Enter SPENCER.

SPENCER:

> Fly, lord! There is no time to eat.
> May I call your army to battle?

EDWARD:

> No, Edward knows his men are off at home.

SPENCER:

> You will not fight against Lord Mortimer?

EDWARD:

> God help me. Fighting is his element.

Off with SPENCER *and* SOLDIERS. *Behind the scenes soldiers break camp.*

Battle, flight.

Enter MORTIMER, ANNE, YOUNG EDWARD, TROOPS.

ANNE:

The God of kings confers success in battle
On those who fight in the very shadow of right.
Since we're successful, therefore right, give thanks
To Him Who moved the stars in their courses for us!
We're come thus armed into this part of England
To stop a breed, more abandoned than the others,
Uniting strength with strength, from rampaging here,
Bloody with our own steel and butchering
Our own bodies!
As the frightful case of poor seduced King Edward
        shows—

MORTIMER:

My lady, if you wish to be a soldier,
You may not show your passions in your words.
The face of the isle is changed, because today
The Queen of England landed with her son!

Enter RICE AP HOWELL.

RICE AP HOWELL:

A following wind is bearing the king toward Ireland,
On a tiny vessel, abandoned by the people.

MORTIMER:

May the wind drown him or leave him in the lurch.
Lords, now that we control this kingdom
From the Irish sea across to the English channel
Raise the young Edward on a shield and let
The whole camp swear allegiance to him!
Show our chief public servant to his soldiers!

YOUNG EDWARD *is carried out. All off except* MORTI-
MER *and the* QUEEN.

ANNE:

> Now he has his Scottish troops and now
> His bitch comes and leaps on him, what is left
> Of him: half-eaten kitchen leftovers
> And a hemp bed all in holes. My body, though,
> Begins to perk up like a virgin's!

MORTIMER:

> Troops must be sent down south.
> Tomorrow evening you must be in London.
> Still no news from the Irish fleet.
> It'll come in soon, I hope. You're tired?

ANNE:

> You're working?

MORTIMER:

> Making England safe for you.

ANNE:

> Oh, Mortimer, there's less pleasure than I thought
> In tasting the fruit of this victory.
> It's stale in the mouth, it's watery, it's
> No joke.

MORTIMER:

> Are you thinking of Edward?

ANNE:

> Why should I? I don't know him any more.
> But that's his smell here in the tent.
> Better to be in the Scottish hills than here
> In the swampy lowlands.
> What do you think to offer me, Mortimer?

MORTIMER:

> You're surfeited already, and your bloated
> Flesh pines for London.

Enter BALDOCK *with the drink.*

> Who are you, man?

BALDOCK:

> King Edward's Baldock. I bring something to drink.

MORTIMER (*taking the drink*):
> Hang him!

BALDOCK:
> Don't know if that's what I'd advise, good sir.
> Not that I wouldn't go along, of course:
> It's the most earthy fate and won't take long.
> But my Irish mother would be sorry to see it, sir.
> Leaving the tent, to get him a cup of water—
> For between good and bad fortune there's not time
> To swallow a mouthful of water—I loved him much.
> And now, returning to the tent, my unhappy
> Duty is to betray him.
> For you won't take him without my help:
> I alone have entry to his heart.
> What's more you wouldn't even know him, Madam.
> Even his mother wouldn't, or his innocent son.
> For time and living have quite changed him.

MORTIMER:
> Good. Bring him to us.

BALDOCK:
> The Bible teaches how this may be managed.
> When your people come with manacles and ropes
> I'll say to him: "Dear sir, don't be upset,
> Here is a handkerchief." The man I then
> Give a handkerchief to is him.

Near Harwich.

KENT (*alone*):
> He fled at the first puff of wind. He's sick.
> Why did I take up arms against you so
> Unfraternally?
> Sitting in your tent on their honeymoon
> This guilt-stained pair aims at your life, my Edward.
> God, rain revenge on my damned head!
> Sure as the rain falls down and downhill flows the
>   river

Injustice won't live to be old while justice lives forever.

*Edward is taken prisoner in the granary of Neath Abbey,
19 October 1324.*

Neath Abbey.

EDWARD, SPENCER, ABBOT.

ABBOT:
My lord, don't be suspicious, have no fear.
Forget I was humiliated by you.
The times have changed. In storms like these
Both you and we are but petitioners
To Our Lady of the Shipwreck.
EDWARD:
Any who saw my body, Father, might
Well reflect on how the times have changed.
ABBOT:
Take this pillow as you may wish to hide
From evil eyes here in the granary.
EDWARD:
Not the pillow, Abbot. Leave the soldier
His hempen bed.

Enter BALDOCK.

Who comes?
BALDOCK:
King Edward's Baldock.
EDWARD:
Our only friend. What comfort to the hunted
When a brother seeks him in his hiding place!
Drink our water with us. Eat our salt and bread.

BALDOCK:

> The moon has changed three times since I saw you
> Encamped at Harwich.

SPENCER:

> How are things in London?

BALDOCK:

> Upside down, I gather.

EDWARD:

> Come, Spencer! Baldock, come! Sit down with me.
> Make a test now of the philosophy
> You've sucked from breasts of celebrated wisdom
> In the works of Plato and of Aristotle.
> Oh, Spencer, since words are rough,
> And only part us heart from heart
> And understanding is not granted to us,
> Amid the deafness nothing remains except
> Bodily contact between men. And even
> This is little. All is vanity.

Enter a MONK.

MONK:

> A second ship's been cruising in the harbor.

ABBOT:

> Since when?

MONK:

> The last few minutes.

EDWARD:

> What are you saying there?

ABBOT:

> Nothing, lord. (*To* SPENCER:) Did anyone see you
>   come here?

SPENCER:

> No one.

ABBOT:

> Are you expecting anyone?

SPENCER:
No, no one.

MONK:
The ship is putting in.

BALDOCK:
Tell me, King Edward, when Roger Mortimer
Was in your hands at Killingworth
Why did you spare him?

EDWARD *is silent.*

Today you'd have a following wind to Ireland.
And if you were in Ireland, you'd be saved.

SPENCER:
The wind left us in the lurch, it almost
Drowned us.

EDWARD:
Mortimer?
Who speaks of Mortimer? A bloody man!
Upon your bosom, Abbot, I lay this head
Weary of grief and of brutality.
Would that my eyes might never open!

BALDOCK:
What's that noise?

SPENCER:
Nothing. The snow-wind.

BALDOCK:
I thought a cock crew. Must have imagined it.

SPENCER:
Open your eyes, my lord! This sleepiness
Betokens nothing good, Baldock. We are betrayed
Already.

Enter RICE AP HOWELL *with* TROOPS.

SOLDIER:
I'll bet all Wales it's them.

BALDOCK (*to himself*):
> Just look who sits there hoping that he can
> Escape unseen—as if flies covered him—
> These murderous hands!

RICE AP HOWELL:
> In England's name: who among you is the king?

SPENCER:
> There's no king here.

BALDOCK (*goes over to* EDWARD):
> Please take this handkerchief, dear sir:
> There's sweat upon your brow.

RICE AP HOWELL:
> Hold that man. It's he.

> EDWARD, *going, between armed men, looks at* BAL-DOCK.

BALDOCK (*weeping*):
> My mother in Ireland has to eat!
> Lord! You must pardon me!

In Shrewsbury Castle the captive King Edward refuses to abdicate.

Shrewsbury.

ABBOT, *now Archbishop of Winchester,* RICE AP HOWELL.

ABBOT:
> When he succeeded Edward Longshanks he
> Had his good time with a certain Gaveston,
> Who baptised me once with gutter water in
> A murky alley near Westminster Abbey.
> And then, in consequence of an error, he
> Took a madman's oath, became a tiger.
> Somewhat later, along with many others,
> The Queen left him.
> She had loved him very dearly for a time.

Several years passed before I saw him again.
Shipwrecked he was, and stained with vice and blood.
He was under my protection in Neath Abbey.
Today I am Archbishop of Winchester
Successor to a man whom he beheaded
And am commissioned to demand from him
His crown.

RICE AP HOWELL:

Now he's a captive. He
Refuses food and drink. Be gentle with him:
You are speaking to his heart and not his head.

ABBOT:

When you hear me say "Permit me to begin"
Draw nearer with some others to bear witness
To the abdication of King Edward the Second.
Painless and imperceptible I'd make
The king's concession, draw it from him like
A rotten tooth.

Enter EDWARD.

RICE AP HOWELL:

He talks all the time. Listen to him and say
Nothing. Talking is better for him than
Thinking. He warms himself with words, believe me.
Bear in mind that he is cold.
Won't you eat something? Why do you refuse
To eat, my lord?

EDWARD *is silent.* RICE AP HOWELL *leaves.*

EDWARD:

The wounded deer
Runs for a plant that closes up the wound
But when the tiger's flesh is torn, the tiger
Digs deeper into it with savage claw.
I often think all's in a state of flux.
If I remember that I am a king, I think
I should have vengeance for misdeeds against me

Which Mortimer and my Queen committed,
Although we kings, when all our power is gone,
Are but sharp shadows on a sunny day.
I think, certainly, that much is vanity.
The peers rule and I am called the King
And my unfaithful Queen,
Repulsive to me once because she clung
To me like some loyal lapdog,
One on whom love does not
Grow naturally like the hair on her head,
But is a thing that changes with what changes,
Stains the marriage bed
While Care stands at my elbow and while Sorrow
Holds me to his bosom and I bleed
At all the changing. At such times
I could wish to be a peasant in a hut.

ABBOT:

God paints with grief and pallor, sir, the faces
Of those he loves. Would it please your highness to
Unburden your breast into my priestly ear?

EDWARD:

I squeezed taxes from the fishermen of Yarmouth
When they were starving.

ABBOT:

What else weighs on your conscience?

EDWARD:

I kept my wife in town one whole dry August
—Thirteen fifteen. It was a whim.

ABBOT:

What else weighs on your conscience?

EDWARD:

That I spared Mortimer for the wicked pleasure
It gave me to do just that.

ABBOT:

What else weighs on your conscience?

EDWARD:

I whipped my dog Truly till it bled. From pride.

ABBOT:
> And what weighs on your heart besides?

EDWARD:
> Nothing.

ABBOT:
> Not unnatural vice? Or bloody deeds?

EDWARD:
> Nothing.
> Oh, savage misery of man's condition!
> Say, Father, must I now give up the crown
> To make the wicked Mortimer a king?

ABBOT:
> You're much mistaken, lord. The crown's requested
> Respectfully for Edward's little head.

EDWARD:
> And yet it is for Mortimer, not Edward,
> Who's just a lamb between two wolves who will
> All of a sudden have him by the throat.

ABBOT:
> He's in God's hands, this child, in London,
> And many say your abdication would
> Be good for him and you.

EDWARD:
> Why do you tell a lie to one who's hardly
> Strong enough to open his eyes? In the
> Face of my weakness say it fearlessly:
> You do this so that England's vine* will die
> And Edward's name stand in no chronicle!

ABBOT:
> Recent times must have been harsh indeed, my lord,
> That you insist on man's iniquity
> So obdurately. Since you have opened
> Your heart to me, my son, now once again
> Lay your head in my bosom and listen.

EDWARD *lays his head in his bosom.*

---

* Emblem on the British crown.—*E.B.*

Take off your crown, your heart will be lighter,
    Edward.

EDWARD (*takes off the crown; then*):
    Let me wear it just today! You should stand
    Near me till it's evening, and I'll fast
    And cry: "Shine on, O sun! Don't let the black
    Moon take possession of England!
    Stand still on the shore, ye ebb and flow! Stand still!
    Ye moons and seasons all, stay where you are
    So that I can stay king of lovely England!"
    For such a day goes swiftly.

He puts the crown on again.

    Inhuman creatures, fed with tiger's milk,
    Lust for their king's downfall.
    Look this way, beasts, from Westminster Abbey!
    I can't get it off, my hair comes with it,
    The two have grown together! Oh, it was ever
    A slight burden to bear like the slight crown
    Of the maple tree, charming, a slight burden ever,
    And now forever a little thin blood,
    A scrap of skin and some quite dark blood
    Will stick to it, left over from King Edward's
    Powerlessness and poverty, the tiger's booty.

ABBOT:
    Restrain yourself. This is the green discharge
    Of the flesh's mortification.
    It's deceit, it's wind and rain of night.
    Open your shirt at the neck,
    I'll lay my hand upon your heart which can
    Beat the lighter, because my hand is real.

EDWARD:
    If it were real, and all this too were real,
    The earth would open wide and swallow us up!
    Yet, since it does not open, and so since
    It's a dream, deceit, and nothing to do with

This world's quotidian reality
I now take off the crown!

ABBOT:

Yes! Tear it off! It's not your flesh!

EDWARD:

Sure that this is not real because I must
Wake in Westminster Castle in London town
After thirteen years of war that ended well:
I, Edward, King of England, in
The registry of christenings at Carnarvon,
And son of Edward Longshanks in the papers
Of the church.

ABBOT:

Have you broken out in a sweat? You must eat.
I'll put the crown where you cannot see it.
But be quick!

EDWARD:

Are we in a hurry? Here,
Take it then. Grab it.
But in a cloth if you don't mind, it's wet.
Hurry! Hurry! It's almost evening. Go!
Tell them Edward at Shrewsbury did not wish
To eat the snow-wind among wolves
And gave this in return for a roof in winter
Which was at the door.

ABBOT:

Permit me to begin:
I, Thomas, Archbishop of Winchester,
Ask thee, Edward of England, second of that name,
Son to Edward Longshanks: Art thou willing
To leave the throne and to renounce
Thy rights and claims of heretofore?

RICE AP HOWELL *and others have entered.*

EDWARD:

No! No! No! You lowdown cheats! You liars!
Would you measure the ocean with your little

Measuring cup? Did I talk too much?
Did I venture out on the ice?
Did you come here this time without a storm, my
    man?
Are you wearing different clothes now, Abbot?
I had one face of yours cut off, didn't I,
Winchester? Faces of the kind multiply
In a way that gives us problems.
Like fleas, a certain Mortimer would say
In such a case. Or did your face come off
When I washed you in the gutter, so that I
Didn't see it when I threw my head upon
Your bosom? No, Abbot,
The things of this earth are not durable.

ABBOT:

Don't fool yourself. Your hand might be too good
To touch my face, but that face none the less is real.

EDWARD:

Go! Quick! It's evening. Tell the peers
Edward will soon be dead.
Less haste would be more polite.
Say too he bade you
When they ring the bells for him
Not to mourn him overmuch
Yet that he begged you to go down on your knees
And say: it's easier for him now. Say that
He asked us, on account of his insanity,
Not to believe him when he uttered something
That sounded like surrender of the crown.
For three times over he said: No.

ABBOT:

My lord, it shall be as you've said. For us,
Only concern for mother England moves us.
When they
Sought someone who was not your enemy
No one was found but me in two whole days.
With this we take our leave.

Off, with the others, except RICE AP HOWELL.

EDWARD:
> Now give me some food, Rice ap Howell,
> For now Edward eats.

He sits and eats.

> Now I've not abdicated, the next thing
> They'll bring to me will be my death.

Enter BERKELEY *with a letter.*

RICE AP HOWELL:
> What's that you've got there, Berkeley?

EDWARD:
> We know.
> Excuse us, Berkeley, that we're eating now.
> Come, Berkeley, pour your message on
> My naked heart.

BERKELEY:
> Do you believe, my lord, that Berkeley
> Would stain his hands?

RICE AP HOWELL:
> An order from Westminster lays down
> I must resign my office.

EDWARD:
> And who must guard me now? You, Berkeley?

BERKELEY:
> That is what's ordered.

EDWARD (*taking the letter*):
> By Mortimer whose name is written here.

He tears the letter up.

> May his body like this paper be torn in pieces!

BERKELEY:
> Your grace must ride to Berkeley straight away.

EDWARD:
> Wherever you wish. All places are alike
> And any earth is fit for burial.

BERKELEY:
> Do you think Berkeley is cruel?

EDWARD:
> I do not know.

In the years 1324-1326 the captive King Edward passes from hand to hand.

Shrewsbury.

RICE AP HOWELL (*alone*):
> His condition aroused my pity. That is why
> Berkeley had to drag him away.

> *Enter* KENT.

KENT:
> In London it is said he abdicated.

RICE AP HOWELL:
> A lie.

KENT:
> Mortimer says it.

RICE AP HOWELL:
> He lies. In my hearing he said three times over: No.

KENT:
> Where *is* my brother?

RICE AP HOWELL:
> Berkeley took him to his place thirteen days ago.

KENT:
> London believed he was here with you.

RICE AP HOWELL:
> Berkeley received an order signed by Mortimer.

KENT:
> Strange that none saw the king face to face.

Strange that none heard his voice and strange that
    now
He only speaks from the lips of Mortimer!

RICE AP HOWELL:

It is certainly strange.

KENT:

I'll ride forthwith in haste to Berkeley
From Edward's lips to sort out truth from lies.

Queen Anne laughs at the world's emptiness.

Westminster.

QUEEN, MORTIMER, *the* GURNEY TWINS.*
MORTIMER:

Did Berkeley give him to you willingly?

ELDER GURNEY:

No.

ANNE (*aside*):

Between these tapestries in Westminster
It stinks of slaughtered hens.
The Scottish air was easier on you.

MORTIMER (*in talk with the* GURNEYS):

You see, this Berkeley was a man with milk
In his bones. He wept at the drop of a hat.
Need only see someone having a tooth out
And he'd swoon on you.
May the earth lie lightly on him!
You're not that kind, I trust?

ELDER GURNEY:

Oh no, my lord, we're not like that at all.

ANNE:

Business propositions!
A stench of too much history between
These walls of Westminster! Won't the

---

* Though the text below calls them the elder and the
younger.—*E.B.*

Skin come off your hands in London's lye?
Your hands are a scribe's hands.

MORTIMER:

Where is your prisoner?

YOUNGER GURNEY:

Northeastwestsouth of Berkeley, my.lord.

MORTIMER:

Look, there are people whom fresh air
Won't hurt. Know any geography?
Could you teach someone about England who
Knows her too little?
England northeastwestsouth?

ELDER GURNEY:

Should we take him all over the place?

MORTIMER:

Mainly where no people are or sun.

ELDER GURNEY:

Good, my lord, we are your men.

ANNE:

Ale! Ale!
Jonah sat and waited for Nineveh's promised end.
Only God didn't come back that way that time
So Nineveh *didn't* end. And yet
I've eaten splendidly and am full of food
And can hold more of it than when
I was a growing girl. Did you ever
Look into metaphysics, Mortimer?

MORTIMER:

There are people, of course, who talk all the time.

YOUNGER GURNEY:

We are quite different people.

MORTIMER:

Did you ever read a chronicle?

ELDER GURNEY:

No, no.

MORTIMER:

That will be all.

Both GURNEYS *leave.*

We have a wolf by the ears which—if
It escapes—will pounce on us.

ANNE:

D'you sleep badly? See white shapes at night?
Often? Just bed sheets, Mortimer, nothing more.
Caused by dyspepsia.

MORTIMER:

When his name comes up, the Commons are moist-
    eyed.

ANNE:

The man I suppose you're talking of is silent.

MORTIMER:

Because he's stubborn and won't talk one must
Out-lie the lies with lies.

ANNE:

Business propositions!
These Westminster days pass too slowly, and
There are too many of them.

MORTIMER:

In the catechism, husband-murder
Comes after parent-murder.

ANNE:

You can get letters of indulgence.

MORTIMER:

With your legs open and your eyelids closed
Snatching at everything, you're insatiable, Anne.
You eat in your sleep. You call out in your sleep
Things that will be my death.

ANNE:

I sleep, you mean. How will you wake me?

MORTIMER:

With Westminster bells and bared teeth. For
Before the noses of the incredulous peers
You've got to crown your son in haste.

ANNE:

Not my son, please!

Not that child
Suckled with she-wolf's milk in weeks when she
Was vagrant, wandering through the swamps
And hills of gloomy Scotland,
Not that child
So innocent to look at
Too much night on his eyelids
Entangled in the savage net with which
You go fishing!

MORTIMER:

Hoisting a small load out of the primeval
Slime—my own strength ebbing with the years—
I can't help seeing, stuck to it,
The human algae. More and more.
As I pull myself upwards I
See ever more dead weight.
Around the knees of the last one, another
Last one. Ropes of people. And at
The pulley-wheel of these ropes, breathless,
Dragging them all up: me.

ANNE:

Name the faces of your human algae.
My husband Edward? My son Edward?

MORTIMER:

You.

ANNE:

Long fearing that my arms, debilitated,
With which I held a human being upright
Would one day fail, I can see clearly now
Where age mixed weariness in the blood of my veins:
What now remains of
That crude expedient of outstretched arms
Is an empty prehensile mechanism.
I am old and tired, Roger Mortimer.

Enter YOUNG EDWARD.

MORTIMER:

Hook up your dress, Anne, do not let your son

See your over-ripe flesh.

YOUNG EDWARD:

Remove this third party from your sight,
Mother: we wish to talk with you.

ANNE:

Mortimer's your mother's prop and stay, child.

YOUNG EDWARD:

I want you to give me some news of my father.

ANNE:

If your mother hung the perilous decision
Upon your lips, child, tell me, would you go
Along with her into the Tower
If through the coloring of your answer
That is the way the dice should fall?

YOUNG EDWARD *is silent.*

MORTIMER:

You show restraint, you're clever, Edward.

YOUNG EDWARD:

Mother, you should drink less.

ANNE *laughs.* YOUNG EDWARD *leaves.*

MORTIMER:

What are you laughing at?

ANNE *is silent.*

Let us prepare
The coronation of this boy in haste.
Our dealings will have quite another look
When they are covered by a monarch's name.

ANNE:

Whatever's happened, and whatever will,
—Heaven will either forgive it or it won't—
I like the taste of your blood
And I won't leave you till the roof falls in.
Meanwhile write, underwrite, give orders,
As you think fit.
I'll sign anything you want.

She laughs.

MORTIMER:

What are you laughing at this time?

ANNE:

I'm laughing at the world's emptiness.

Highway.

KENT (*alone*):

Berkeley is dead, and Edward's disappeared,
And Mortimer, ever bolder, claims, in London,
Edward renounced the throne in Berkeley's hearing.
And Berkeley's dead and cannot comment. For
Us sons of Edward Longshanks the light grows dim,
Yet there've been signs the skies might brighten yet.
The Commons were disturbed. They demanded
An account of the ex-monarch's whereabouts.
Many referred to him as poor King Edward.
In Wales the people have been murmuring
Against the butcher Mortimer. Yet maybe
Only the crows and ravens know the dwelling
Of England's Edward. And I've dared to hope
That my repentance might not come too late!
But who is that poor creature among the pikes
And lances?

EDWARD *enters, the two* GURNEYS, SOLDIERS.

YOUNGER GURNEY:

Hey! Who's that?

ELDER GURNEY:

Take a look at him: it's his brother Kent.

EDWARD:

Oh, noble brother, help me, set me free!

ELDER GURNEY:

Part them. Off with the prisoner!

KENT:

Soldiers! Let me put a question to him!

YOUNGER GURNEY:
> Stop his mouth up!

ELDER GURNEY:
> Shove him in the ditch.

> EDWARD *is taken off*.

KENT (*alone*):
> Edward! Did you abdicate? Edward! Edward!
> Woe to us!
> They drag the King of England like an ox.

*3 December 1325: The mighty Earl Roger Mortimer is
hard pressed by the peers on account of the king's dis-
appearance.*

Westminster.

MORTIMER, QUEEN, ABBOT, RICE AP HOWELL.

ABBOT:
> My lord, a rumor's growing now like cancer
> That Edward did not abdicate.

MORTIMER:
> At Berkeley, in Lord Robert Berkeley's hearing,
> He abdicated voluntarily.

ABBOT:
> At Shrewsbury, in my own hearing,
> Edward shouted: No.

RICE AP HOWELL:
> As he did often in my presence.

ABBOT:
> It would be useful if Lord Berkeley would
> Bear witness upon oath in the House of Commons
> How, before whom, Edward resigned the crown.

MORTIMER:
> I've had news today of Berkeley:
> He's on his way to London.

RICE AP HOWELL:
　　And where's the king?
MORTIMER:
　　At Berkeley, where else?
　　Much knowledge, Rice ap Howell, diminishes
　　The appetite. Since I quit books and knowledge
　　I sleep much sounder and digest my food.
RICE AP HOWELL:
　　Only where is Edward?
MORTIMER:
　　I know nothing of your Edward. I don't
　　Love him, I don't hate him, nor does he haunt
　　My dreams. In matters that concern him
　　Go to Berkeley, not to me! You yourself,
　　Winchester, were against him.
ABBOT:
　　The church went the way God went.
MORTIMER:
　　Which way was that?
ABBOT:
　　With the winner, Mortimer.

Enter KENT *with* YOUNG EDWARD.

KENT:
　　It seems my brother's not in Shrewsbury now.
MORTIMER:
　　Your brother is in Berkeley, Edmund.
KENT:
　　It seems that he is not in Berkeley now.
MORTIMER:
　　Since Harwich, rumors have taken to growing
　　Like sponges in the rain.
ANNE:
　　Come to your mother, child.
MORTIMER:
　　How goes it with the honorable Kent?

KENT:

>In health, Lord Mortimer. And you, my lady?

ANNE:

>Well, Kent. It's a good time for me, I'm quite
>Content. I went fishing last week in Tynemouth.

MORTIMER:

>There was a time when fishing in Tynemouth would
>Have been very much in a certain person's line.

ANNE:

>Will you come fishing in Tynemouth next week, Kent?

MORTIMER (*aside*):

>You eat too much and don't chew it, Anne.

ANNE (*aside*):

>I eat, drink, and make love with you.

ABBOT:

>What did you say about Berkeley, my lord?

MORTIMER (*to* KENT):

>You were missed in London three whole weeks.

KENT:

>I rode across this ravaged country
>And with misgiving saw my brother's tracks.

YOUNG EDWARD:

>Mother, do not persuade me to be crowned!
>I will not do it!

ANNE:

>Be content. The peers demand it.

MORTIMER:

>London wants it.

YOUNG EDWARD:

>Let me talk with father first, then I'll do it.

KENT:

>Well spoken, Ed!

ANNE:

>Brother, you know it is impossible.

YOUNG EDWARD:

>Is he dead?

KENT:

>In London one hears many things. I'm sure
>You must know something, Roger Mortimer.

MORTIMER:

>Me?
>In Little Street, in the bright noonday sun,
>Five sharks were seen going to a tavern
>For some ale. Later, slightly high,
>They were seen kneeling in Westminster Abbey.

KENT:

>They were praying for Berkeley's soul.

MORTIMER:

>O fickle Edmund: do you now wish him well?
>You who were the cause of his arrest?

KENT:

>Cause now to make it good.

YOUNG EDWARD:

>Yes! Yes!

KENT:

>Ed, do not let them talk you into things.
>Don't take the crown off your father's head.

YOUNG EDWARD:

>I don't want that, either.

RICE AP HOWELL:

>He doesn't want that, Edward.

MORTIMER (*takes the* YOUNG EDWARD, *and carries him to
the* QUEEN):

>Tell your son Edward, my lady, that
>England is not accustomed to permit
>Contradiction.

YOUNG EDWARD:

>Help, Uncle Kent! Mortimer's trying to hurt me!

KENT:

>Hands off England's royal blood!

ABBOT:

>In this confusion, would you really crown him?

MORTIMER:
    As the law dictates.
RICE AP HOWELL:
    As you dictate.
ABBOT:
    Then I ask you, in the name of the law,
    In the presence of the man's own son, wife, brother:
    Did King Edward abdicate?
MORTIMER:
    Yes.
ABBOT:
    Your witness?
MORTIMER:
    Robert Berkeley.
KENT:
    Who is dead.
RICE AP HOWELL:
    Berkeley is dead?
KENT:
    Has been for seven days.
RICE AP HOWELL:
    Did you not say you heard only today
    He was on his way to London?
ABBOT:
    Since your witness, Mortimer, left this world
    A week ago, or two days ago, with your permission
    I'll ride to Berkeley to clear all this up.
KENT:
    In Berkeley you'll find blood on the floorboards
    But not the king.
RICE AP HOWELL:
    Didn't you say the king was at Berkeley?
MORTIMER:
    I thought he was.
    Time pressed. The rebels in Wales have kept us busy.
    When time has passed and we have greater leisure
    Much will be clarified.

ABBOT:

> It means your leading witness, Berkeley, is silent
> While your second witness, Edward, has disappeared?

MORTIMER:

> And though I have to cast a great fish net
> Over the whole island, I'll find that witness.

KENT:

> Search your own army then, Mortimer.
> Among their pikes and lances I saw my brother
> Driven along the highway by a mob.

ABBOT:

> Did your brother speak to you?

RICE AP HOWELL:

> You're very pale, my lord.

KENT:

> His mouth was gagged. What, do you think, Arch-
> bishop,
> Would that mouth have testified?

MORTIMER:

> So he did not abdicate? You lie!
> I invoke martial law:
> Off with this man's head!

YOUNG EDWARD:

> My lord, he is my uncle. I won't allow it.

MORTIMER:

> My lord, he is your foe. I order it.

KENT:

> You need *my* head too, butcher Mortimer?
> Where's the head of Edward Longshanks' *eldest* son?

ABBOT:

> He's not in Berkeley, not in Shrewsbury.
> Where is he now, Roger Mortimer?

YOUNG EDWARD:

> Mother,
> Don't let him do away with Uncle Kent!

ANNE:

> Ask nothing of me, child. I may not speak.

KENT:

> Would you consult the murderer
> About the murdered?
> Look in the Thames, look in the Scottish woods,
> The resting place for him who found no place
> To hide, since he held back with his teeth the word
> That you so need.

RICE AP HOWELL:

> Where is the man today, Lord Mortimer?

ABBOT:

> Did he abdicate?

MORTIMER:

> Summon the Commons on February eleventh.
> From his own lips Edward will then confirm
> His resignation. But as for me,
> Reaping suspicion where I sowed but thanks,
> Prepared at all times to submit my heart
> And every hour I've spent in Westminster
> For God to look at,
> Handing my office back to you as Queen,
> Returning to those books, my sole true friends,
> Which I exchanged some years back for
> The mess of war and the world's disapproval,
> Before the peers and you I now accuse
> The son of Edward Longshanks, Edmund Kent,
> Of capital High Treason. I demand his head.

ABBOT:

> You go too far.

MORTIMER:

> It rests with you, my lady.

ANNE:

> My verdict is:
> You are banished, Edmund Kent, from London.

KENT (*to* MORTIMER):

> You'll pay dear for this.
> Gladly Kent takes his leave of Westminster

Where he was born and where today
A lustful wench is living with a bull.

ANNE:

Earl Mortimer, you're still the Lord Protector.

ABBOT:

I'll call the Commons for February eleventh
That this poor Edward may himself, forsooth,
Make known to all of us the naked truth.

All leave except MORTIMER.

MORTIMER (*alone, letting in the* GURNEY TWINS):

Bring him to the point where he says yes
To every question. Burn it into him.
But be in London on February eleventh.
You have carte blanche. He must say Yes.

*After an absence of fourteen years King Edward sees the
city of London once again.*

Just outside London.

EDWARD, *the two* GURNEYS.

ELDER GURNEY:

Don't look at us so thoughtfully, my lord.

EDWARD:

Ever since you came, whenever the night falls,
You take me overland. Where must I go now?
Don't go so fast. Because I'm eating nothing
I'm full of weakness, my hair falls out.
My senses swoon at the stench of my own body.

YOUNGER GURNEY:

Are you in a good humor then, lord?

EDWARD:

Yes.

ELDER GURNEY:

> We're coming to a pretty big town now.
> Will you be glad to see the Eel?

EDWARD:

> Yes.

YOUNGER GURNEY:

> Are not those willows, lord?

EDWARD:

> Yes.

ELDER GURNEY:

> The Eel doesn't like unwashed visitors.
> There's gutter water. Please sit down and we
> Will shave you.

EDWARD:

> Not gutter water.

YOUNGER GURNEY:

> You want us to shave you with gutter water?

They shave him with gutter water.

ELDER GURNEY:

> The nights are getting shorter now.

YOUNGER GURNEY:

> Tomorrow's February eleventh.

ELDER GURNEY:

> Wasn't it a certain Gaveston who got you in trouble?

EDWARD:

> Yes. I remember that Gaveston very well.

YOUNGER GURNEY:

> Stand still.

ELDER GURNEY:

> Will you do everything you're told?

EDWARD:

> Yes. Is this London?

YOUNGER GURNEY:

> This is the city of London, lord.

11 February 1326.

London.

SOLDIERS *and mob, before Westminster.*

FIRST SOLDIER: February eleventh will be a real big day
    in the history of England.
SECOND SOLDIER: A night like this is enough to freeze
    your toes off.
THIRD SOLDIER: And still seven hours to stand here.
SECOND SOLDIER: Is Eddie in there yet?
FIRST SOLDIER: This is where he's got to cross into Parlia-
    ment.
SECOND SOLDIER: Westminster's lit up now.
THIRD SOLDIER: Will the Eel bring him around?
FIRST SOLDIER: I'll bet a silver shilling on the Eel.
SECOND SOLDIER: I'll bet two shillings on Eddie.
FIRST SOLDIER: What's your name?
SECOND SOLDIER: Smith. And yours?
FIRST SOLDIER: Baldock.
THIRD SOLDIER: It'll certainly snow before morning.

Westminster.

EDWARD, *muffled, the two* GURNEYS.

ELDER GURNEY:
    Are you glad to be in the Eel's place?
EDWARD:
    Yes. Who's the Eel?
YOUNGER GURNEY:
    You'll see.

    The two GURNEYS *leave. Enter* MORTIMER.

MORTIMER:
    The sweaty marketplace that's London
    Has brought things to this pass: my head

Hangs, you could say, upon these minutes, and
On the Yes and No of humiliated lips.
I'll pull this Yes out like a tooth. He's weak.

EDWARD *removes the covering from his face.*

EDWARD:
Is this Westminster and are you the Eel?
MORTIMER:
They call me that. It is a harmless beast.
You're tired. But you shall eat, drink, even bathe.
Like to?
EDWARD:
Yes.
MORTIMER:
You'll choose yourself a friend.

EDWARD *looks at him.*

You will be borne to England's Parliament
And there you'll testify before the peers
That you have abdicated.
EDWARD:
Come nearer, Mortimer. You may sit down.
But on account of our badly-shaken health
Pray make it short.
MORTIMER (*to himself*):
He proposes to be hard.
Antaeus-like he draws strength from the soil
Of Westminster.
(*Aloud.*)
Brevity is the salt of watery soups.
It's a matter of your answer
As to your possible abdication
In favor of your son.
EDWARD:
After thirteen years away from Westminster
And long campaigns and thorny exercise
Of high command
My body's need has led me to a sober

Concern with that same body's growth and its
Decay.

MORTIMER:

I understand.
Night journeys, human disappointments
Make one think many thoughts.
And midst this weariness of which you speak
And which you bear with patience
And midst the badly-shaken health you also speak of
Do you still intend to continue in office?

EDWARD:

That is no part of our plans.

MORTIMER:

Then you'll say Yes?

EDWARD:

That is no part of our plans.
The air of these last days begins to clear.
Edward, whose fall approaches—
It is inevitable but not frightening—
Knows himself. And though he does not long
To die, he knows the usefulness of shrinking
Annihilation.
Edward, who is not poor Edward any more,
Pays readily with his life for whatever pleasure
A strangler can afford him.*
But come ahead, Mortimer, if the hour is ripe—

MORTIMER:

You're hideously entangled in yourself,
While I
Who lost the taste for ruling years ago
Bear on my back this island
Which one workaday word from you would snatch
From civil war.
Maybe lacking in feeling, but knowing a lot,
Not royal certainly, but maybe just,

---

* Hercules strangled Antaeus to whom Mortimer has just
compared Edward.—*E.B.*

And not even that if you insist, but only
The rough and stammering mouth of poor old
    England,
I ask, I even beg, that you
Abdicate.

EDWARD:

Don't bring your wretched claim to me.
And yet it gives me pleasure
Now my body's fate is settled
To see your hands at my throat.

MORTIMER:

You fight well.
As one who knows good orators
And whom they call the Eel
Respecting your good taste
I request from you none the less
In this little transaction of ours
At a late hour of the night
A succinct answer.

EDWARD *is silent.*

Don't close your ears!
Lest the weight of a human tongue or
The whim of the moment
Lest, finally, misunderstanding
Should hurl this England into the Atlantic,
Speak!

EDWARD *is silent.*

Will you, today, at noon, before the Commons,
Abdicate?

EDWARD *is silent.*

Will you *not* abdicate? Will you refuse?

EDWARD:

Although Edward must now bring to a close
Affairs more complex than those known to you,
My busy Mortimer,

Yet none the less
Since he is still in this world
He will avoid
As far as your affairs go—which at this
Increasing distance seem to him quite grisly—
The presumption of uttering
One word.
For your question, then, he has
Nor Yes nor No.
From this time forward,
His lips are
Stitched together.

Westminster.

MORTIMER *(alone)*:

As long as he draws breath, it can come to light.
Since raw wind cannot tear from his back
The ridiculous mantle, nor can mild sun lure
It off, let it go with him into
Decomposition.
A strip of paper, carefully prepared,
Odorless, proving nothing, will set up this
Contretemps.
If he knows neither Yes nor No to my question
I shall know how to answer him in kind.
"Eduardum occidere nolite timere bonum est."
That's with no comma. They can read it:
"Kill Edward you must not, fear it!"
Or according to the state of their innocence,
And whether they've been eating or fasting:
"Kill Edward, you must not fear it."
"Kill Edward you must not fear it"
Without any punctuation, thus.
I'll send it that way.
And now
England is under us and

God is over us and God
Is very old.
I'll go before the peers, my own sole witness.
Lightborn, come out.

Enter LIGHTBORN.

If your captive when dawn dawns
Has still learned nothing he is
Unsalvageable.

Cloaca in the Tower.

The two GURNEYS.

ELDER GURNEY:
   He's talking all the time tonight.
YOUNGER GURNEY:
   It's a miracle how this king won't ripen.
   Unnaturally exhausted, since,
   When he tries to sleep, our drum beats,
   He's standing in a hole, up to the knees in
   Sewage water—for all the privies in the Tower
   Are emptied out there—and won't say Yes.
ELDER GURNEY:
   It's extraordinary, brother. A while ago
   I opened the trap door to throw him meat
   And was almost stifled by the odor.
YOUNGER GURNEY:
   His body has more staying power than ours.
   He sings. If you open the trap, you hear him singing.
ELDER GURNEY:
   I think he's writing Psalms because it's spring.
   Open up. We can ask him again.
   Wanna say Yes, Eddie?
YOUNGER GURNEY:
   No answer.

Enter LIGHTBORN.

He isn't ripe yet.

LIGHTBORN *hands over his paper.*

What's this? I don't get it.
"Kill Edward you must not fear it."

ELDER GURNEY:

It says: Kill Edward.

YOUNGER GURNEY:

Give the sign.

LIGHTBORN *gives it.*

ELDER GURNEY:

There's the key, there's the lock.
Carry out the order. Need anything else?

LIGHTBORN:

One table. One featherbed.

YOUNGER GURNEY:

Here's a light for the cage.

Both GURNEYS *leave.*

EDWARD:

The hole they keep me in's the cesspool.
Upon my head has fallen for seven hours
The offal of London.
But such water hardens my limbs: which are now
Like cedar wood.
The stench of excrement gives me boundless great-
    ness!
And the good sound of the drum keeps me awake,
Though weak, so death won't find me fainting but
Waking.
Who's that? What's that light? What do you want?

LIGHTBORN:

To comfort you.

EDWARD:

You want to kill me.

LIGHTBORN:

> Why does your highness mistrust me so?
> Come out, brother.

EDWARD:

> Your looks are all death.

LIGHTBORN:

> I'm not without sin.
> I'm not without heart either. Just
> Come over here and lie down.

EDWARD:

> Howell had pity. Berkeley was poorer but
> Did not stain his hands.
> The heart of the elder Gurney is a mountain
> In the Caucasus.
> The younger Gurney's harder yet.
> Mortimer is ice. You come from him, don't you?

LIGHTBORN:

> You're overtired, lord.
> Lie on this bed and rest a while.

EDWARD:

> Rain was good. Not eating filled the belly.
> But the best was the darkness.
> All were irresolute, many reluctant, but the best
> Betrayed me. Therefore
> Who is dark, let him stay dark,
> Who is unclean, let him stay unclean.
> Praise deficiency, praise cruelty, praise
> The darkness.

LIGHTBORN:

> Sleep, lord.

EDWARD:

> There's something buzzing in my ear that whispers
> If now I sleep I'll never wake. It's
> Expectation that so makes me tremble.
> Yet I can't keep my eyes open, they're glued
> Together. And so tell me why you came.

LIGHTBORN:

> For this.

Chokes him.

Westminster.

MORTIMER (*alone*):
>Dawn then, February eleventh! Compared to me
>What are these chaps but highwaymen?
>They tremble at my name and do not dare
>Connect that name with his death.
>Let them just try to!

>*Enter the* QUEEN.

ANNE:
>Oh, Mortimer, my son already knows
>His father's gone, and, hailed as king,
>Comes here knowing also you and I
>Were the murderers.

MORTIMER:
>What if he does know? He's a child
>So tender that a drop of rain would kill him.

ANNE:
>He went to Parliament to ask support
>From the peers who, like the people, have been
>   waiting
>Since early mass to see the man you promised:
>His father.
>He wrings his hands, he tears his hair, swears oaths.
>He'll be avenged on us both.

MORTIMER:
>Do I look like a man who'll soon be six feet under?

ANNE:
>Our sun is setting, Mortimer.
>Oh, look, he's coming, and they're with him!

>*Enter* YOUNG EDWARD, ABBOT, RICE AP HOWELL,
>PEERS.

YOUNG EDWARD:
>Murderers!

MORTIMER:
    What's that, my child?
YOUNG EDWARD:
    Don't hope your words can scare me now.
ANNE:
    Edward!
YOUNG EDWARD:
    Mother, stay out of this.
    If you'd loved him as I did
    You wouldn't have stood for his death.
ABBOT:
    Why don't you answer my lord the king?
RICE AP HOWELL:
    At this hour Edward was to have spoken
    In Parliament.
A PEER:
    At this hour Edward's mouth is mute.
MORTIMER:
    What man connects *me* with this death?
YOUNG EDWARD:
    This man.
MORTIMER:
    Your witness?
YOUNG EDWARD:
    My father's voice in me.
MORTIMER:
    Have you no other witnesses, my lord?
YOUNG EDWARD:
    Those who're not here shall be my witnesses.
ABBOT:
    The Duke of Kent.
RICE AP HOWELL:
    Berkeley.
A PEER:
    The Gurney twins.
ABBOT:
    A man named Lightborn, seen in the Tower.

ANNE:

Stop!

ABBOT:

Who bore a paper with your writing on it.

The PEERS *examine the paper.*

RICE AP HOWELL:

Ambiguous by all means. There's no comma.

ABBOT:

On purpose.

RICE AP HOWELL:

Could be. But it doesn't state
That an order was given to do away with the king.

YOUNG EDWARD:

O Mortimer, you know it happened.
And it shall happen to you: you die!
A witness in this world that your all too
Cunning cunning
Through which a royal body ended in a hole
Was too cunning for God.

MORTIMER:

If I understand you right, you're accusing me
Of murdering Edward the Second.
Sometimes the truth's improbable and never
Can one predict on which side the wild bull
—The State—will next roll over. Any spot it
Does not roll over on's considered moral.
The wild bull has rolled over; and on me.
If I had proofs, what good would they do me?
If a State
Were to call a man a murderer, such a man
Would be well-advised to act
Like a murderer, though his hands
Were white as Scotland's snow.
So I've held my tongue.

ABBOT:

Ignore the convolutions of the Eel!

MORTIMER:

> Take the seal from me. Spit
> Squadron on squadron at the Île-de-France.
> In Normandy our armies are just rotting:
> Send me to Normandy as Governor.
> Or as a Captain. Recruiting Sergeant. Tax Collector.
> Who d'you have, after all, who whips your armies on
> Against the foe, thus, with his naked arms?
> Only don't—
> Between dinner and wiping your lips with your nap-
> kins—
> Hurl me headlong downwards thus and all
> Because a young animal's bleating for blood
> At the death of his animal father!
> Would you still say
> It is the time to clear up Edward's case
> Even if, in purging a single murder, you
> Cut loose this island from its moorings and
> It sails away on a sea of blood?
> You need me.

Pause.

> Your silence can be heard all the way to Ireland.
> Got another language between your teeth since yes-
> terday?
> If there's no blood on your hands, then there
> Is still no blood on your hands.
> To be coolly disposed of thus—ah, well,
> Such is morality.

ANNE:

> For my sake, spare Lord Mortimer, son.

YOUNG EDWARD *is silent.*

> Be silent then. I never tried to make
> A talker of you.

MORTIMER:

> Madam, stay out of this. I prefer an end
> To begging for life from a milky boy.

YOUNG EDWARD:

Hang him!

MORTIMER:

There is, my lad, and the slattern Fortune turns it,
A wheel. It bears you upwards with it.
Upwards and upwards. You hold tight. Upwards.
Then comes a point. The high point. From it you
    can see
It's not a ladder. It bears you downwards.
It's round after all. Who has seen this
Does he fall or should we rather say that he
Arranges to fall?
An entertaining question. Think it over!

YOUNG EDWARD:

Take him away!

MORTIMER *is led off*.

ANNE:

Don't have the blood of Mortimer on your head!

YOUNG EDWARD:

Those words prove, mother, that you maybe too
Have my father's blood on your head.
Linked with Mortimer
You too are suspect, and we send you
To be cross-questioned in the Tower.

ANNE:

Such a death's-head joke as that you did not
Suck up with your mother's milk, third Edward.
Hard-pressed more than most, and not from any liking
For change as such, I saw injustice always
Feeding its man and rewarding with success
Every conquest of conscience.
But even injustice let *me* down.
You tell me there died a few hours ago
One whom the sight of you reminds me of
Faintly, and who gave me pain, and whom
I forgot (which was kind of me, you might say),
Got rid of his face, even, and his voice,

Entirely. The better for him.
His son now sends me to the Tower which
Will be as good as other places.
You, who can be excused for looking with
A child's eyes into hard and bygone things,
What do you know of the world
In which there's nothing more unhuman than
Cold judgment and cold justice?

Off.

YOUNG EDWARD:
It remains
To bring King Edward's corpse to worthy rest.
ABBOT:
And none of those who'd seen the coronation
In Westminster Abbey also saw
The funeral of this second Edward who
Not knowing, as it seemed,
Which of his foes remembered him
Not knowing
What lineage was above him in the light
Not knowing
The color of the leaves upon the trees
Not knowing
The seasons, the positions of the stars
Forgetting
Even himself
Died
In misery.
YOUNG EDWARD (*while all kneel*):
That our lineage may not suffer for these sins,
O God, grant us remission at this time
And grant us, God, that also
Our lineage may not perish in the womb.

THE TIME SCHEME. Marlowe avoids dates, but gives the impression that the action of his play encompasses about one year. Brecht puts a date at the head of each sequence of scenes and spreads the whole action over a period of nineteen years. However, since the story Brecht tells is even further removed from actual history than Marlowe's there is no question here of strict accuracy in point of time. If Brecht likes to give not only the year but the month and day, it is for a chronicle *effect*—the poetry of history, as it were—and not because a historian had fed him the details. There is something here that is especially characteristic of Brecht, as the present translator can verify from having been invited by him to go to the New York Public Library and hunt up documents on which the scenes of his *The Private Life of the Master Race,* already written, might *seem* to have been based. Had this been done, scenes like *The Jewish Wife* would have been printed, no doubt with year, month, and day, as dramatizations of newspaper reports, though in fact they were not.

Marlowe seems to have read about Edward II almost exclusively in Holinshed's *Chronicles.* Brecht and Feuchtwanger may well have read about him exclusively in Marlowe and/or the German translations of Marlowe. Holinshed, being, then, a kind of ultimate source for both plays, it may be of interest to indicate summarily Holinshed's own time scheme:

1305: Gaveston banished for persuading Prince Edward
    to break into the Bishop of Coventry's Park. Prince
    Edward imprisoned.

1307: Coronation of Edward II. Gaveston's return.
    The Bishop of Coventry imprisoned. Gaveston gets
    married.

1308-1309: Gaveston again exiled; is recalled.

1312: Gaveston insults the lords, is captured and exe-
    cuted.

1322-1323: Edward defeats and executes the Barons.
    Mortimer is imprisoned and escapes.

1323-1324: News of disasters in France.

1325: Edward sends the Queen to France as ambassadress.

1326: She joins forces with Mortimer and returns to England with an invading army. The King, defeated, escapes to Neath Abbey.

1327: The King is taken to Kenilworth (Killingworth), abdicates, is placed in Berkeley's charge; is murdered.

1330: Mortimer executed.

The time scheme brings up the question whether Marlowe's or Brecht's play is closer to Brecht's (later) idea of Epic Theatre. On the face of it, Marlowe's is: his play is far more episodic and wide-ranging. To a great degree, Brecht goes to work like any other early twentieth-century (or even nineteenth-century) adaptor, simplifying, eliminating, reducing the action to certain central encounters and carefully prepared climaxes. His play is far more "logical." No longer does Mortimer merely "escape": he is let go for reasons central to the theme and characterization. No longer are Edward's whereabouts accidentally noted, at a critical juncture, by a peasant: they are given away to his enemies by a Judas. If Marlowe ties the threads of the story far more closely together than Holinshed or history had done, Brecht ties them far more closely than Marlowe, so that finally Gaveston, Edward, the Queen, and Mortimer are a thoroughly integrated group—a cast of characters for an intimate modern play.

On the other hand, Brecht's story covers a period nineteen times as long. And since the passage of this much time is thrust on the audience's attention, we are obviously meant to grasp its implications. For example, we get thirteen years of Gaveston, instead of Marlowe's month or two. This Gaveston is a tremendous piece of Edward's life, no plaything of a moment. (That Young Edward must have been born during the Gaveston period is perhaps something we are not meant to realize; and one wonders if Brecht did). Secondly, the passage of nineteen

years leaves its mark on Edward. This fact plays a part in
the plot itself: he is protected from detection by becom-
ing completely unrecognizable to his old associates, and
this is what makes the Judas figure (Baldock) necessary
to them. More important still, the new, positive Edward
of the final sequence really has time to come credibly into
being. (In Marlowe there are only a couple of hints of
such a new man. On the whole, those critics are justified
who have said that his "hero" is pitiable only because
such things shouldn't be done to anyone. "It Should Happen to a Dog" would be an appropriate modern title for
the older play.) In one respect, Brechtians might take *Edward II* as a finger exercise for *Mother Courage*. There is
a comparable attempt to show human deterioration in
theatrical terms, and *Edward II* is also a play which begins
with banners streaming and ends in filth and beggary. As
for structure, one of the ideas of Epic Theatre is that
natura facit saltus, nature does make jumps, and very
bold in this play are some of the leaps in time from one
sequence to the next—as from 1311 to 1320 at one point
but, just as daringly at another, from 1320 to 1324.

LIGHTBORN'S BRAVER WAY. The word Lucifer means "light
bearer," and Lightborn is the Lucifer of *Edward II*. (Harry
Levin has pointed out that one of the devils in the Chester
cycle had already been called Lightborn.) How does he
kill the king? In the Brecht, he asphyxiates him, presumably with the aid of the feather bed and the table he
has asked for. Marlowe spells out this action thus:

> So, lay the table down, and stamp on it,
> But not too hard, lest that you bruise his body.

But when first consulted, Lightborn has seemed to favor
other approaches:

> 'Tis not the first time I have killed a man.
> I learned in Naples how to poison flowers;

> To strangle with a lawn thrust through the throat;
> To pierce the windpipe with a needle's point;
> Or whilst one is asleep, to take a quill
> And blow a little powder in his ears:
> Or open his mouth and pour quicksilver down.
> But yet I have a braver way than these.

Is the "braver way" the way of the table and feather bed?
In itself, it hardly seems a comparable procedure. Rather,
one is tempted to see in this line an allusion to what
Holinshed says actually happened. (And we know Holin-
shed did not invent it, since there is an earlier record.)
After telling that when attempts were made to poison
Edward, the king got rid of the poison "by purging either
up or down," Holinshed continues:

Whereupon when they saw that such practices would not serve
their turn, they came suddenly one night into the chamber
where he lay in bed fast asleep, and with heavy feather beds
(or a table as some write) being cast upon him, they kept him
down, and withal put into his fundament an horn, and through
the same they thrust up into his body a hot spit (or as others
have through the pipe of a trumpet, a plumber's instrument of
iron made very hot) the which passing up into his entrails,
and being rolled to and fro, burnt the same, but so as no
appearance of any wound or hurt outwardly might be once
perceived.

Now this procedure is hardly suitable to the theatre, and is
not followed by Marlowe except in respect of the table
and bed, while Lightborn is not to be found in Holinshed
but would seem to have been imported by Marlowe from
medieval dramatic tradition. Are not the name and character of Lightborn Marlowe's carefully chosen substitute
for the unusable chronicle account? By this is meant not
only that what "they" did to Edward was "diabolical" in
a general sense but that it was precisely diabolical in so
hideously suiting the punishment to the crime? Edward
was guilty of sodomy—perhaps not in Holinshed's eyes,
but certainly in Marlowe's. The devil now buggers him

with a red-hot skewer, and he does this in such a way
that there will be no surviving evidence. It seems like a
myth of society's vicious attitude to homosexual acts:
cruelly punishing them, slyly duplicating them, and then
affecting innocence and detachment.

MORTIMER'S SONG. The song sung by Brecht's Mortimer is
found in Marlowe but only *spoken* and that not by Mortimer but by Lancaster:

> And thereof came it that the fleering Scots   18 pi
> To England's high disgrace have made this jig:
>
> Maids of England, sore may you mourn,
> For your lemans you have lost at Bannocksbourn,
> With a heave and a ho!
> What weeneth the King of England,
> So soon to have won Scotland?—
> With a rombelow.

Scholars have traced it back to Fabyan's *Chronicle* (1533)
where we read:

This song was after many days sung in dances in the carols
of the maidens and minstrels of Scotland to the reproof and
disdain of English men, with divers other which I overpass.

It is inconceivable that any of Marlowe's noblemen would
burst into song. The image of a singing Mortimer is
emphatically Brechtian and prepares for such things as—
many years later—a dancing Creon.

"Bannocksbourn," more commonly known as Bannock-
burn, is the site of the famous battle of 1314 in which
the Scots, under Robert the Bruce, routed Edward II's
English army. "Bannockbride" is, presumably, a Brechtian
invention: one should not expect this Scotland to be any
closer to the actual thing than the England of *The Three-
penny Opera* or the America of *Jungle of Cities*.

ENGLISH–GERMAN–ENGLISH

Any English translator of Brecht's *Edward II* has to decide what use, if any, he is going to make of lines, phrases, single words out of Marlowe's *Edward II*. Readers of the Introduction to this volume, and of the Notes at the back, will have no difficulty figuring out why so little use was made of Marlowe by the present translator. And besides the points made in these other places there is this to say: the German translations of Marlowe are not of the Elizabethan period but either of the nineteenth or the early twentieth century. Hence, when Brecht mixes "Marlowe" with Brecht no one is going to notice the mixing process: all the German is from one period. When, on the other hand, an English or American translator mixes his own work of 1965 with Marlowe's of 1592 everyone is going to notice two "strata," as it were, of text. Such a procedure is impossible. A homogeneous result must be attempted. That is why I did my work on this play without a copy of Marlowe on my desk, without rereading his play at all, indeed, until a complete, if unrevised, modern text had come off the typewriter. This is not to say that I tried to get rid of all Elizabethanisms. Being impossible anyway, such a result was hardly to be attempted. Yet the reader is spared deliberate, noticeable quotation from Marlowe.

I reread Marlowe afterward, and changed a very few lines of my own text where the Marlowe reading was simply better without being perceptibly Marlowe. The edition of Marlowe's play that I used (and drew upon for my Introduction) was that of H. B. Charlton and R. D. Waller as published by Methuen. On the Brecht text I received help and advice from Dr. Hugo Schmidt. The translation was first made in Berlin during the winter of 1964–1965. In October 1965 it was produced by the Actor's Workshop of San Francisco, and I made a number of changes on the basis of that production: my thanks to the producers, Ken Kitch and John Hancock, for making this possible.

                            —E.B., *New York, Autumn 1965*